T0042999

VAN GOGH'S EAR

Poetry for the New Millennium

Issue Number 2

Volume 2, Number 1

Spring 2003

COMMITTEE ON POETRY • NEW YORK
FRENCH CONNECTION PRESS • PARIS

FOUNDER & EDITOR:
Ian Ayres

ASSISTANT EDITOR: Vincent van Dongen • DESIGN & LAYOUT: Ian Ayres
PUBLIC RELATIONS & EVENTS: Jennifer Chen • SALES: Peter Hale
COMPUTER GURUS: Thomas R. Thorpe, Antoine Loakira
ADMINISTRATION: Bob Rosenthal, Eric Elléna • WEBSITE: Daniel Auster
ACCOUNTING: Kay Spurlock, Sandrine Surget • SHIPPING: Ahmat Adoum Nassar

Many thanks to the whole team!

Cover painting © Van Gogh Museum, Amsterdam (Vincent van Gogh Foundation)

Van Gogh's Ear *is a joint publication of*
Committee on Poetry (New York) and French Connection Press (Paris)

COMMITTEE ON POETRY
P. O. Box 582, Stuyvesant Station, New York, NY 10009 U.S.A.

FRENCH CONNECTION PRESS
12, rue Lamartine, 75009 Paris France • www.frenchcx.com/vangoghsear

Spring 2003   Vol. 2, No. 1

Printed in France
ISBN 2-914853-01-7

"The whole course of human history can be seen as a constant struggle to expand the definition of who is 'us' and shrink the definition of who is 'them.'"

—Bill Clinton
December 19, 2002

"Gardez cet objet précieusement."

—Vincent van Gogh
December 23, 1888

Vincent cuts off his ear on a Sunday evening, two days before Christmas. At 11:30 p.m., he arrives at brothel number 1, asks for Rachel, and hands her his ear, saying, "Keep this object carefully." He then disappears. The police find him at home the next day, lying in bed, apparently lifeless.

Contents

Sam Abrams

THE OLD POTHEAD'S SPRING LIST

go view Hendrick's and dead
Shreela's dogwood blooms
always two weeks ahead
of ours

get two packs orange Zig-Zag papers

drop canned food off
at Catholic Worker

drop Windows keyboard and floppies
at Pastors for Peace
for Cuba Caravan

remember what Barbara Ehrenreich
said "in the Sixties
the people with power
were acting irresponsibly
so the people without power
had to begin to take responsibility"

and what Robert MacNamara confesses
speaking for the powerful
"we were wrong, terribly wrong"

"there are facts lodged in the world"
says Baraka,
"lodged"
like seeds

Dannie Abse

A FIGURE OF 8

In Mr Theophilus's jail
of the sun-striped classroom
the boy half listens to a story
of royalty-loving Christopher Robin.
Then, after musical scales,
(his friend, Fatty Jones, is scolded
Fatty Jones is sobbing)
sings, "Let the prairie echo,
God bless the Prince of Wales."

Free, at last, arms horizontal,
he jet-roars out of school
into a vigorous sunset,
soars between the Hs
of the Millennium Stadium,
loops the loop, flies to Africa
to see naked women
(whom gently he caresses);
turns left at Albany Road,
farts H2 Ss.

The evening's shot down in flames
butchers' reds in the clouds are dark,
smoke is rising from the drains,
someone has bombed the park.

Both the swings are on fire,
the empty see-saw is charred;
the enemy is a brute,
the enemy must be foiled;
blood is streaming down the chute,
the wooden horses are running wild.

There's a furnace in the churchyard
(a sorcerer has cast his spell)
the mandrake's screaming and the yew,
the graves are sinking down to hell.

Unseen, a spaceship from another world
flees the heights, drags a spooky trace.
Below the pond is poisoned and the dew.
Safely the boy comes home to base.

There beneath the night's first star,
observed by his patient cat,
he chalks across the garden shed
FUCK WINNIE THE POOH.
Then adds for luck and Fatty Jones
FUCK MR THEOPHILUS TOO.

LEIS DE CON

Companho, tant ai agutz   d'avols conres
qu'ieu non puesc mudar non chan   e que no.m pes;
Enpero no vueill c'om sapcha   mon afar de maintas res.

E dirai vos m'entendensa   de que es:
no m'azauta cons gardatz   ni gorcs ses peis,
ni gabars de malvatz homes   com de lor fitz non agues.

Senher Dieus, quez es del mon   capdels e reis,
qui anc premiers gardet con   com non esteis?
C'anc no fo mestiers ni garda   c'a si dons estes sordeis.

Pero dirai vos de con   cals es sa leis,
com sel hom que mal n'a fait   e peitz n'a pres:
si c'autra res en merma qui.n pana,   e cons en creis.

E silh qui volran creire   mos casteis
anho vezer pres lo bosc   en uin deveis:
per un albre c'om hi tailla   n'i naison dos ho treis

E quam lo bocx erstaillatz   nais plus espes,
E.l senher no.n pert son comte   ni sos ses;
A revers planh hom la tala   s.l dampn....

Tortz es ca....dan noi a....

Guillaume IX of Acquitaine (1071-1127)
—Translated by **W. D. Snodgrass**

THE LAWS OF CUNT

Friends, I've had such sorry times,   such country fare,
  That I can't help singing songs   of deep despair;
Though my private small affairs   shouldn't get blabbed everywhere.

Still, I'll open all my thoughts   for you at once:
  I don't care for fishless ponds   or guarded cunts
Or the boasts of gutless wonders   who've gone slack on all the fronts.

Mighty Lord, great King of all   this universe,
  He who first set guards on cunts   should die accurst.
There's no servant or protector   ever served his lady worse.

I'll speak out concerning cunt   to state its laws,
  Since I've done wrong and borne worse   to serve its cause:
Take from most things, they're decreased; cunt's   bounteous as it was.

Anyone who thinks this counsel   is not much good,
  Find some private thicket grown   out near the wood;
Cut down one tree—two or three more   spring up where the old one stood.

Trim back brush and the woods flourish   more and more;
  Then their lord has no less than   he had before—
Since there's been no loss or damage,   what's the man complaining for?

It's plain wrong to cry you're injured   when there's no loss to the score.

13

Louis Armand

PERVIGILIUM VENERIS

thrust up into the root, stub-fingered, blackening a hole
you still haven't
located—all winter shrank
like a plastic doll &
one freakish, paralytic eye—sleep
is the fixedness of a
hidden culpability; the trussed eaves where tongues
turn viscous, the
ear humid—mordant nights passed in
self-ridicule, a flaccid
imago nailed to the inside of an
elongated mirror—the horror show
winds on, its
intricate banality of painted
corpses, cropped out with teeth: to
decorate the fringes, pretexts
for intervention
in the normal viewing schedule—cramped, airless
cubicles in which
a captive mind masturbates itself
towards extinction: a
tedious dénouement that always ends with the replay
button, caught in a loop
which flesh itself could only ever
approximate

ALL MESSAGES HAVE BEEN PLAYED

A chance encounter—he'd
dropped a stitch somewhere along the way
to a palimpsest. Put it all there
and then wonder why it was done?

You don't need to die there.
A freshet is ever restless,
the stars coming undone in a way
thought to be magic before there was magic,

dim process of stars.
It seems to have gone back
to doing what it was doing all along.
Maybe we'll enjoy these together.

There were more of us
then, when we seemed so few.
This plenteous space confined us—
an afternoon of succulents, hens and chicks,

the rusted roadster. The waterfall *is* the window.
You can see through it. Still more of us.
Have her meet you at the party for the residents.
But the poetry—how do you handle it?

Paul Auster

NOTES FROM A COMPOSITION BOOK
1967

1

The world is in my head. My body is in the world.

2

The world is my idea. I am the world. The world is your idea. You are the world. My world and your world are not the same.

3

There is no world except the human world. (By *human* I mean everything that can be seen, felt, heard, thought, and imagined.)

4

The world has no objective existence. It exists only insofar as we are able to perceive it. And our perceptions are necessarily limited. Which means that the world has a limit, that it stops somewhere. But where it stops for me is not necessarily where it stops for you.

5

No theory of art (if it is possible) can be divorced from a theory of human perception.

6

But not only are our perceptions limited, language (our means of expressing those perceptions) is also limited.

7

Language is not experience. It is a means of organizing experience.

8

What, then, is the experience of language? It gives us the world and takes it away from us. In the same breath.

9

The fall of man is not a question of sin, transgression, or moral turpitude.
It is a question of language conquering experience: the fall of the world
into the word, experience descending from the eye to the mouth. A
distance of about three inches.

10

The eye sees the world in flux. The word is an attempt to arrest the flow,
to stabilize it. And yet we persist in trying to translate experience into
language. Hence poetry, hence the utterances of daily life. This is the
faith that prevents universal despair—and also causes it.

11

Art is the *mirror of man's wit* (Marlowe). The mirror image is apt—and
breakable. Shatter the mirror and rearrange the pieces. The result will
still be a reflection of something. Any combination is possible, any
number of pieces may be left out. The only requirement is that at least
one fragment remain. In *Hamlet*, holding the mirror up to nature amounts
to the same thing as Marlowe's formulation—once the above arguments
have been understood. For all things in nature are human, even if nature
itself is not. (We could not exist if the world were not our idea.) In other
words, no matter what the circumstances (ancient or modern, Classical or
Romantic), art is a product of the human mind. (The human mimed.)

12

Faith in the word is what I call Classical. Doubt in the word is what I call
Romantic. The Classicist believes in the future. The Romantic knows that
he will be disappointed, that his desires will never be fulfilled. For he
believes that the world is ineffable, beyond the grasp of words.

13

To feel estranged from language is to lose your own body. When words fail
you, you dissolve into an image of nothingness. You disappear.

Ian Ayres

THE ALARM IS SET

It is 4:13 a.m. I've awakened
On the brink of World War III
This pain in my gut could be cancer
Could be gas could be mass extinction
Setting in getting centered having entered
Through my brains what scientists say
Unanimous the gig is up there'll be
No more new slang no more history
To claim historic awakenings

They—They say, "We have entered
A period of mass extinction
Not seen since the age of the dinosaurs,
An emerging global crisis that could have
Disastrous effects on our future food supplies,
Our search for new medicines, and on
The water we drink and the air we breathe."
They say, "Humans are still destroying
Biodiversity at an unprecedented rate."

I'm among the rich indifferent to the light
Bulbs I burn—each with a switch I flick
Casting my vote on and off for extinction
The faith I cling to a mere block of ice
Containing car exhaust and ozone
A polar cap melting into polluted air
Conditioning has made money my god
Defined by the corporations I buy into
I wear myself like a billboard

TRANSVESTITE

No idea what I've been doing last twenty years putting on her clothes while she's
    shopping visiting or like today at Sheila's Beauty Salon my wife who'll be
    home any minute
When she walks in I'll be a nymphomaniac on our black velvet bedspread orgasmic
    in her smoke blue see-through negligée draping me hirsute in aphrodisia
    stroking her ready-to-burst brassière or running my hands down to her plum
    lace panties throbbing with manhood fingering her garters holding her silk
    stockings smooth to my thighs
Such attire arousing me since fourteen when I played Peeping Tom with a cousin
    two years older than I watching her take off pink panties for string bikini
    I ran to the lake diving in hiding my stiff shame under water
At dusk I stole those soiled undies pressed them to my growing cock reliving her
    furry vulva stepping out of the pink cotton I sniffed inhaling her breathing her
    made me want to slip them on *be in them* lying on my stomach rubbing
    against garment and bed I ejaculated
Surrounded by increasing amounts of my cousin's clothing I was in her string bikini
    the day my mom swung open the door disgust on her face calling me a sicko
    calling my cousin to see
Both tried to humiliate by making me wear my cousin's dress my cousin making up
    my face like a woman's as Mom left bored with the game my cousin noticing
    my erection slapping at it through the dress the whole scene a permanent itch
    in my psyche a secret fetish to be exposed
And now my wife opens the bedroom door drops purse staring hairdo fresh clutches
    fur coat as I in feminine whisper explain loving her gender more than male
    how I long to share my female side as her eyes catch my arousal straining
    her panties obvious beneath our favorite negligée
She could scream for divorce call the police have a breakdown how little I know her
    arching a thin penciled brow peeling out of chinchilla her frosted lips spread
    stepping toward making me a masochist shivering ready for those upraised
    lacquered claws to bloody my rouged and powdered cheek
Instead scented sweet as I she palms a caress our ample breasts heaving
    in soul-searching time my glossy red lips claimed equal in a tongue-filled kiss
    fondling each other's delicate lace and silk like lesbians in love
    beautiful lesbians in love

Charles Baudelaire

LE LÉTHÉ

Viens sur mon cœur, âme cruelle et sourde,
Tigre adoré, monstre aux airs indolents;
Je veux longtemps plonger mes doigts tremblants
Dans l'épaisseur de ta crinière lourde;

Dans tes jupons remplis de ton parfum
Ensevelir ma tête endolorie,
Et respirer, comme une fleur flétrie,
Le doux relent de mon amour défunt.

Je veux dormir! dormir plutôt que vivre!
Dans un sommeil aussi doux que la mort,
J'étalerai mes baisers sans remord
Sur ton beau corps poli comme le cuivre.

Pour engloutir mes sanglots apaisés
Rien ne vaut l'abîme de ta couche;
L'oubli puissant habite sur ta bouche,
Et le Léthé coule dans tes baisers.

A mon destin, désormais mon délice,
J'obéirai comme un prédestiné;
Martyr docile, innocent condamné,
Dont la ferveur attise le supplice,

Je sucerai, pour noyer ma rancœur,
Le népenthès et la bonne ciguë
Aux bouts charmants de cette gorge aiguë
Qui n'a jamais emprisonné de cœur.

Charles Baudelaire
—Translated by *Ulick O'Connor*

LETHE

Rest on my heart, cruel and sullen one.
Adored tigress, monster of indolent air,
I long in the thickness of your tawny hair,
To plunge my trembling fingers till I'm done.

To bury the burden of my aching head
In the perfume of your towering skirts,
Like a withered flower, to savour though it hurts
The sweet odour of a love that's dead.

Rather than live, for sleep my body longs
To slip into a slumber sweet as death.
I shower remorselessly kisses with each breath
Upon your body with its gleam of bronze.

Nothing can equal your bed's abyss
To engulf and soothe my bitter cries;
On those lips deep oblivion lies,
And all Lethe surges through your kiss.

From now on I shall act as Fate requires,
And use the unhappiness from which it stemmed,
A willing martyr and innocent condemned,
Who fuels his agony with his own desires.

I shall drink to drown my rancour for a start,
Nectar, sweet hemlock and the rest
From the ravishing tips of your erect breast
Which never once has held a captive heart.

Bill Berkson

SIGNATURE SONG

Bunny Berigan first recorded "I Can't Get Started"
with a small group that included Joe Bushkin, Cozy Cole
and Artie Shaw in 1936.
Earlier that same year, the song,
written by Ira Gershwin and Vernon Duke,
and rendered as a duet patter number by Bob Hope and Eve
Arden, made its debut on Broadway in *The Ziegfeld Follies*.
By 1937, when Berigan re-recorded it in a big-band setting,
"I Can't" had become his signature song,
even though, within a few months, Billie Holiday would record
her astonishing version backed
by Lester Young and the rest of the Basie Orchestra.

Lovers for a time, Lee Wiley and Berigan began appearing
together on Wiley's fifteen-minute CBS radio spot,
Saturday Night Swing Club, in 1936.
Berigan died from alcoholism-related causes on June 2, 1942.
Although "I Can't Get Started" is perfectly suited to Wiley's
deep phrasing and succinct vibrato, she recorded the ballad only
once, informally, in 1944, during a Los Angeles club date.
The Spanish Civil War started in 1936 and ended in 1939
with Generalissimo Francisco Franco's forces entering Madrid.
"I've settled revolutions in Spain" goes Gershwin's lyric, just as odd.

[corrected version, 2003]

TANGO
for Liz Rideal

Maybe we need another word for nature
    would chaos do
largely friendly lately it has been a confidant
    up there with actuality, another word that insists on being

    all leaves and unfigure-out-able turnings
      a fork holds up the air sky
its trident mirror image jabs over eons into the
                deep dark snuggle

    That wanderer's length is a bird-colored
      click on deliquescence
         shave off the finer hairs
  you might find a face

    dismissive of skepticism
      an opaque residue
    where fibers lunch on
circular bugs, or vice versa, affinity, figure and ground

         coterminous with
      a sapling dressed to the nines to dissemble
    launching a lecture or panel discussion
      on troubled paradise

lightning strikes but once, from the ground up
    I like to sit in its lap
      the stellar urgency of this life
  actual in less than date and time

Charles Bernstein

SHOULD WE LET PATIENTS WRITE DOWN THEIR OWN DREAMS?

You are in an oblong cylinder that
projects endlessly in front of you.
Handprints line the upper right
arc with an insistent but inconsistent
reiteration. Lances or spears seem
to appear in mid-air, like floaters
in the sun at the beach, and it is
very damp, damp with a faintly
metallic taste. A pool of water
comes up to your ankles but your
shoes are totally dry. You call out—
to your left, right, left, right—
but you're not marching and no one
is giving any orders. The light
is tinted the color of rust but
has no source. You fall to what
you almost want to call the ground
and push forward on your stomach.
You feel anxious but after a while
the lack of expectation and the warmth
of the water, which leaves your clothes
as dry as if you were wearing a wet
suit, is unexpectedly reassuring. When
the light turns white you find yourself
sitting on a chair with a notebook and
pencil in hand.

Anselm Berrigan

A POEM FOR PATRIOTS

shadow stretched stoop walking
mercy clinic rewired concussive consciousness
an interactive scientific luxury item
weirder than imagination as if to let you spy
on my detention post-diction
shadow of an activist martini
inducing opinion ain't listening
primate contam trained frites to sing
vengeance songs on diamonds attacked
for every set of undeclared attacks bonding
via slaughter, paying told being what about that
pain of too much tenderness (insert narrative)
cheap production bursts with alliterative verse heads
my most modern free trade zone has a legal hate gesture
to send in seed bred in the good will tube
I know I can't afford this style
without protectionist policies
can I pay you to read this more dead there than
here story pinned to my name like a good
little fucker of the times
occasional gratuity loves the forced and eternal
coupling, actually I loved the harmlessness
of yesteryear according to many crushable heads
another jealous commie bitches the blues
in fields of daisies the poems then growed
up blood soaked, imported parts
sucking bluebells out of tubas

Anselm Berrigan

SABOTAGE

On with the jalapeño Christmas lights! It's only the end
of July, no calls, no poems, damn this antenna. To defy
being positioned I indulge in irrelevant cosmic lunch
openings, take a handful at my will & dirty this penny-
ante heart. The hub is searching for its head, which is
a lost cause. It was a leaf on the windshield of her car
& she was handed an œuvre. Micro-sized wormholes
dig it, Heidegger's works are at least as manipulative
as Spielberg's. Words spoken by a boot full of wicked
on Brooklyn's vibrating giraffe-ride scene. If François
Villon had ever led a life as sweet as this he wouldn't
give a damn about passing out in Philip Glass' bed.
Whosoever shall encounter him by chance shall read to him
this poem. Who gives a damn about the bathroom door
rotting off its hinges & who gives a damn about a toehold
on a crowded ladder. François does not pity my delusions
nor those of the monks & black-winged demons painted
in gold & tempera onto the panels of my face.

Robin Blaser

from *WANDERS*

mr. & mrs. sew and sew
startled their sewing machine,
there was a mood underfoot
of political and religious despair,
muddy to tread upon
the bolt of cloth for the magnificent
windows twisted, curled on itself
to become glued wallpaper—their
moods were indicative, subjunctive,
imperative—he said—she said
where should we go to give tongue?
if to bark? if tonguing in a bellclapper?
if tonguing in a buckle? if vibrating
the end of a reed? if feathering?
at the tongue of a railway moveable
switch? if tonguing this power?
if tonguing this land? if these days
tonguing and grooving untied tongue-tied
despairs?
        Oh! hearts and minds
who sew their loves—

        Oh! malignant
political and religious stupidity

So, Eros has a mind,

that is where

our vernacular task

began among Troubadours

and Beatrice

was founded   Oh!

discontinuous word order

of love's continuous

adventure writing

between Absolutelies,

figuring *the life*

that is born

in this gap   outside

and inside,   for which

the hyperbaton of this comity

sticks

December 2002

Lee Ann Brown

TRANSFORMATION HYMN

To the tune of "A Mighty Fortress Is Our God"

All Mighty Fortresses Open Your Doors!
All Swords to Ploughshares Beaten!

Why do our Leaders lead us to War—
All vengeful hatred eaten?

For still our ancient foe:
Within us each doth grow—

Our need this hour is great—
Disarm this cruel fate!

Our Words of Love unscrew it!

Dennis Cooper

A SYMPHONY OF CONFUSION
ABOUT THE PEOPLE I KILLED *(for Sue De Beer)*
by Kip Kinkel*

1.

You hate me, or
I only hate you. I
can't tell now, I'm
so complicated.

Things can't hate
things. It's inap-
propriate, I guess,
wanting you dead.

If you hate me, I'm
less myself, I think.
It feels real, but I'm
alone in believing

it's you. You don't
feel it when I do,
since you're not me,
though I hate you

so much, past the
point of realizing
what's you. There's
something here, but

it's not there. Here's
my thing, a thing
where you hate
me, or I believe it.

You shouldn't hate
me so much, as I
said. It makes you
too big of a thing.

Your thing isn't me.
I'm me, and you
won't be anything
if you don't stop.

2.

Why do that? It's disorganized,
and I've been so consistent.
It's too painful to feel, and make
any sense whatsoever. I need

it, although you're hopeless to help.
It likes you a lot, but you don't care,
because you don't even know. I
can't let you see it, or else I'll say

it's for somebody else. If you knew
it was yours, it would scare you off,
like it scares me. You wish. You
didn't do anything to deserve it, I

swear. It's me. I can't keep it inside
with you there. Why do anything
at all? Because you're so happy.
I'm so stupid, evil, and lonely you

don't understand. It's always cold,
and gets colder everywhere when I
feel it. It's such bullshit, but so real.
How can you do that to me? You

don't realize it exists, do you? I
won't let you find out, though I can't
explain why. Call me shit, and leave
me here where nobody knows I'm

alive. By the time you find out, if
you care, you will never believe it
was yours. Until then, it has no
point, which makes everything so

unbelievably hard. I mean in every
way. Why is that a problem?
I can't tell you. How did you do it?
Why confuse me? It's directionless.

3.

I just want to hang out
with you guys like any
person would do but
you put this idea of me
shooting at you in my
head and when you're
shot maybe you'll say
you're sorry we never
hung out but you won't.

4.

How sad that
if I acted like
someone else,
we'd be friends.

That if I had you
as friends, I might
accidentally cause
you to like me.

That being friends
might make you
feel what I feel
now without you.

That you're every-
thing good I've ever
imagined I'd like
more than anyone.

That you are like
you are, being ev-
erything I've ever
wanted to be like.

That I wish you
weren't into the
guys of the type
you hang out with.

That the one thing
that keeps us apart
is a thing we can't
talk about changing.

That I think you'd
agree if I asked,
but if I asked, it
would scare me.

That what I feel
would scare me
when I feel very
kindly toward you.

That I suffer so much
about something
as stupid as you
when I like you.

That to like you
without hanging out
is not to like you,
or even myself.

That because I will
never hang out
with you guys, I can't
like you, I hope.

That if this isn't
true, then I've
never liked anyone
else in my life.

5.

I've figured it out,
I swear. It's our
words, or maybe
mine fueling yours

that you hate, a
pure coincidence.
You say you hate
talking to me, that's

all. So I thought,
That's the way they
put things, and
hating words is to

hate their creator.
But words only
know other words,
when you're not

a psycho. I thought
yours were signals,
like mine. That's
my mistake. It was-

n't hate. That word
is just one of the
syllables you like
to say. It has no

real weight for you,
whereas it's all I've
been saying to you
all along. It's clear

to me now, but it's
so hard to feel. I
say nothing. Or
I just talk to myself.

This poem is me,
and it's nothing but
words about you.
I hope you like it.

6.

To say it, which can't
be. It's under my words,
and hangs out in
a secret headquarter
I can't find to clean.

Why you? It's stupid.
Why not me? It's too
pathetic to talk about,
I feel. How can this
be fake? 'Cos it's not.

To deserve you, it's
so idiotic. I know you
know I wish it were
true, high. Or that you
you were down here.

It keeps coming back,
so rough. I'm not built
well enough to withstand
you. Or you and it, to-
gether at last. Wrong.

Or right. It doesn't
matter, I know. Please
stop, but don't ever
actually stop, I can't
decide. It just isn't.

*Written by Dennis Cooper as Kip Kinkel, the fifteen-year-old student
at Thurston High School (Springfield, Oregon), who was expelled
because he brought a gun to school. Later the next day, he entered the
school cafeteria and opened fire with a semi-automatic rifle, firing
more than fifty shots. During the rampage, Kinkel managed to kill two
fellow students and wound twenty-six others. After police arrested
him, investigators discovered that he had also ambushed and killed
both of his parents as they arrived home. Kinkel was charged as an
adult for the murders at the school and for the murders of his parents.
He was later found guilty and sentenced to over 130 years in prison.

David Cope

TENDER PETALS FOR CALM CROSSING

along this silent path among cliffs thru terraced green you'll
sing beneath your breath where the poet once dreamed

of his escape thru the clouds, where whole populations fled
to rebuild shattered dreams, hands in the moist earth—

stone masons who shaped the rock attentively, that it might
interlock & honor earth that gave both seed & harvest

in the sweep of seasons—ghosts today, they wander with you,
picking your pockets, to know what dreams you bring

to this place, what breath you leave among these rocks,
what song you gather in your backpack & basket of silence:

here, the lost mother weeping for her child borne to minutes
of love before its last breath, the father pouring a lifetime's

devotion thru his hands, his face red with defeated love yet
shining in all the brilliance of that loss—here, the lovers moving

together, their short gasps echoing in a great sigh thru which
another child comes—here, the lost father who could not face

the wreck of his love in his own child's eyes, his sorrow like
a hermit lost in the passes of his own valleys, his heart bursting

with roses he could not bring to his own table—here, warriors
cut down like corn on a day as crisp as this, eyes turning skyward

one last time, up to the light as their blood gushes out on fertile
ground, shining path where arms & legs of the dead clutch

& kick at heaven, vanishing dreams of hungry ghosts. so
you come, bringing blessings & eyes to flush the tears that

still pool in the world's grief thru all the rages of lost centuries,
all the weeping sisters crying for lovers who never appeared,

all the lost brothers marched thru barbed wire to death's
final anonymity in the last bursts they'd ever hear, minds

turned inward to their mother's cries on the day they forced
their way into this light, compassion now for them all:

that your dream be clear when you come to this pass, I send you
this wish where tender petals turn, open in both darkness and light.

STYLE

The object of having a style (as opposed to merely being stylish) is not to be different from other people, but to be more like yourself than nature has made you. A really good portrait is more like you than your own face. Ignore other people. Mr. Sartre says, "Hell is other people." But not if you ignore them.

You must decide who you are and be it like mad. Do not decide on a lot of bizarre mannerisms with which to encrust our self—just as a writer does not decorate boring material with bejeweled phrases (as Mr. Wilde was wont to do). Take away all the words that are irrelevant to your meaning. In other words, style is a process not of accumulation but of denudation.

Mr. Sargent said, "A portrait is a likeness with something wrong about the mouth." But really a portrait is more than that. If you are not spectacular in any way, the unspectacular is your style. You must be able to imagine someone saying to one of your acquaintances, "Come to my party and bring that hum-drum friend of yours." And everyone knows that it means you.

I was asked on one occasion if one could be dowdy and have style, and I thought immediately of Eleanor Roosevelt.

The reason why style is so important is because if you are sure of yourself you do not seize upon a group style—your class, your nationality, your sex. You can avoid this pitfall if you never use the word "we" except to mean yourself and the person to whom you are speaking. It is a mistake to say (or even to think) "we lost a football match"—I didn't lose it, you didn't lose it. Eleven other people that we don't know and have never even heard of us lost it. So, do not go raging through the streets of the Netherlands breaking everything in sight and killing many of the inhabitants.

Stay with it! Never give up!

Gayle Danley-Dooley

DANCING WID DADDY

My Daddy is Fred Astaire
I mean, my Daddy can dance
feet like oars paddling the dancefloor
like it's his Pacific Ocean

I love to dance with my Daddy
I am alive as we V our arms
make fists and pound the innocent air
like butchers
tenderizing the sweetest veal

This man with the gangster, 4ft. brother
(may his gambling soul rest in peace)
Daddy with the asky feet
3 teeth and partial afro hanging on
for dear life

This man who usedta work for the NYFD
(painting hydrants)
tight with his $
loves his 3 children (behind their backs)
had us old
then forgot
only remembering our graduations
and the glory a polaroid can bring

Damn-near 80
But the cancer that chews his prostate
Leaves him alone long enough
For us to turn records into songs
Teddy Pendergrass The Four Tops The Spinners
Daddy and me

It's real pretty
Me and Daddy
Loving each other this way
Spinning, rocking
Not afraid to touch elbows and toetips
Stealing whoops from the crowd
(whoda thought we could move like that)
stomping on the years
with no birthday cards
and letters unmailed

sweating thru the rhythm
bonding inside each beat
no apologies needed
just a moment on the floor
twirling in this light we share
Daddy and me

Savoring our 3 minutes like 2 children
Sucking cherry nowlaters
Never unlocking glances or stopping to sop sweat
From our foreheads
praying this song is the disco-version
taking what's left of our moments together
one step
at a time

BLACK MASS

"It's the signal for the place to really become a complete looney house."
—Henry Miller, *Opus Pistorum*

Henry Miller comes to Paris, wants to see
a black mass like something in *La Bas*
but what he gets is a rank, goat-masked
version of the Folies.
Ten years later, memory gets him
a dollar a page from a Los Angeles
backroom publisher of private deluxe editions.
It keeps him alive that hot summer
before Pearl Harbor, and he tells himself
everything becomes classic someday.
So Miller travels to the fatherland
of his id through a ten-year-old memory,
a call on the old black phone to Opéra 666
(please operator), behind rue de Richelieu,
summer, 1931. Me, I believe him,
somebody who would know showed me
the place last winter, not far
from the old Bibliothèque Nationale.
Miller remembers and types out on a secondhand Underwood
Paris before occupation, magnificently free
of gravity, nothing remotely like New York,
bringing sky down to earth, not earth
to sky. He wrote he liked the way American heiresses got loose
from their vague suppressions and
sexualized their stockings, brushes, jewels
to screw like never in Pittsburgh.
Finally even Mona became defined by
the heavenly arc of Paris,
and after enough years she becomes a movie.
Everything becomes classic.

So in '41 he remembers Ann Alexandra high on heels,
ambergris, and opium as thirteen lower glands raise
the Devil (or at least a stench) in the windowless
hall behind the rue de Richelieu. Diabolical, she kneels
half naked inside a pentagram, red chinoise silk chemise,
pearl sheen stockings, sash of fine lace, so canonical,
spitting in bad French what should have been
Fuck me, Satan, take me but sounds like
Fool me into satin, kick me.
We all get cheated when we want badly in
the physics of imagination and language.
That is the law about libido on Berlitz.
And with a clump and squeak they wheeled
out that painted wood horned and phallused
plaster statue on a trolley to taxi all takers
to hell with a good, hard impelling, so art deco,
so *moderne*, while the Canon, a fat English priest
pushing fifty, tossed around soiled Host and then
sprayed the room as he killed a cock.

All this Miller, stranger on the California coast,
remembers while the sky waits for poetry and rain.
He swallows the pale brandy from hills and slopes
to the north, as he watches movie stars drive by
in convertibles, while in Paris hierophant Adolf
Hitler prepares his own cock to spray wide
some really bad prose and worse porn.

Albert Flynn DeSilver

WE'RE GETTING READY TO RUN OUT OF TIME

I defy the empire

By writing poems

In hemp slacks

While eating an organic

Apple. Americans hate everything

About me except my capacity

For multi-tasking. Picking ears, hemorrhaging in the heart,

Checking e-mail for permanent fatal errors.

I dove through 4 waves then let

Five dive through me.

(Is that a dump truck up your sleeve

Or are you just glad to leave me?)

Today I saw a cell phone in the lobby

Of The Plaza on its hind legs spitting

Through the ear piece at its cheeky handler—

It was a moment of suspended animosity

So I kissed her checkbook.

There are only three people who get me

To the page: Eminem, Mom, Mr. Rogers, and Mom.

Eminem is headlining the Anger Management Tour 2003

Security will be beefed up and sponsored

By Neiman Ranch. Last night I dreamt I set a mirage

On fire and woke up with a charred hole in my pillow—

My coroner doubles as corroborator

Helps me cheat death with protein powder

Implants and a sterling silver hole-puncher.

"I live to punch people full of holes" says my coroner.

ANATOMY

Some words I know: scapula, ventricle, organ, liver, femur.
The body pieced back. The body pieced. The body in

Let's begin simply. Locate the_____

A reference point, as when we stretch our heads back to see clearly the pole
wobbling in the grasp—and the feet? Somewhere, at first beyond vision, the
cornea taking in light, adjusting until the line between tightrope and toe, heel,
ankle, thigh, hip, waist, chest—in, out—neck then head wobbling
eyes eyeing out of sight the white pole

where. we meet. An interstices—two perpendicular lines. Completely still
that instant all eyes fix

together.

As here, his voice behind my own larynx vibrating behind me eyeing the rail, no,
between the rails, the wooden crossties. Eyeing between. My voice eyeing, eyes
eyeing me and it was there, slowing, our train so that

PARMIGIANO CHEESE

One does not—cannot!—go to Parma without bringing back some parmigiano cheese, of course, and thus it was only natural that Massimo Epifani, a native of Otranto, came back from a week-long trip to Parma with an exceptional wheel of parmigiano, aged for three years and weighing no less than 90 pounds. He barged into his house cradling his beloved cheese like a huge baby and, in his excitement, even forgot to kiss his lovely wife, Claretta, who had been waiting anxiously in the living room for at least half an hour to greet him. Although it was not dinner time he insisted on sampling the cheese right away. This was when everything quickly went wrong. According to one version, it was the wife, miffed at not having been kissed at the door, who started to hack at the cheese with a butcher knife, thus provoking her husband into a murderous rage. According to another version, it was the husband who did the cutting. It was his slow, tender handling of the cheese, accompanied by many unctuous comments such as "The cows are very different in Parma" and "You must not *hurt* such a beautiful cheese," that broke his lovely wife's heart and drove her into a jealous fit of retaliation. According to one neighbor, she was heard screaming at the top of her lungs: "Go ahead and kiss that cheese, why don't you?!" Someone then shouted "No no no!" (Or maybe it was "Yes yes yes!") In any case, by the time the carabinieri arrived half an hour later, there were only two pale corpses embracing on the floor, one male, one female, cut up every which way imaginable, lying in a vast pool of blood and cheese.

CLOUDS

I'm trying to find my house on the ground that's
rapidly falling away.
Clouds are complicating things.
The jet climbs into life after death
towards that place where all the longing goes.
Asides turn integral
and what was once freely given
is now gotten by force.
We move into the pitiable stage. The silent phase.
With the loyalty of a doper
and the unerring purpose
of some future poet's dad
pushing a hot dog cart up Fifth Avenue,
the jet has decided to stay
in the air. Today.

Gordon Downie

LOWELL, MASS.

It's cold tonight
in Lowell, Massachusetts.
It's making for more enhanced hearing
among the vice-ridden and the retired
who know a thing or two about
conductive loss.
You get the sense
on a heavily doctored night like this
that in a dream mistaken for prescience
even Kerouac would convert you like a Huron if he could
and get you to say what words can't express:
that powerlessness
with a mathematical bent
colours commentary
into local anaesthetic.

WONDERFUL

I've been watching you - watching the earth freeze - this is wonderful - give me a minute - wonderful - words change in famous poems - cast of millions - give me wonderful before it's to late - it's a wreck and it's to late - call an ambulance - four cells fourier and a diamond - wonderful I say - I keep watching at a distance - usually on a bus and you don't notice - the tires are bald - it's wonderful though - simply wonderful - no murder no crime - just actions without definitions - action that arises - actions that never complete - always cut in half than again - there is no action it's just a definition - the earth is freezing - it's wonderful - the rivers first then the feet - frozen to sidewalks - faces to cement - give me a minute - the words are changing again - it's not the same word that means the same thing - now it's replaced with a different purpose - wonderful though simply wonderful - give me wonderful and we can call it fair exchange - give me wonderful with some change - give me a minute - I'll be watching you - the earth is freezing -

PLEASE PASS THE SALT TOO

bear no responsibility, make atomic detonations blast Zones, Air Pressure Detonators ----------------- Plutonium, Uranium-238, what's best for your money? - the information on how to bubble two fragments; 1.) the nucleus (central mass) 4). Blast Damage ----------------- Everything flammable burns. People burn. [See chart below] In fact, the "Blast-O-Mactic" brand is the best for your money -- One Trident Nuclear Fission/Nuclear Fusion/ Fission (H-Bomb) is a three part sub-atomic vibration of Krypton.

NEXT MONTH'S COLUMN the 'missing' section of three miles away. History Lead Shields and how the fireball began. We here at "Fat Man," destroy 90% fatalities, at a relatively high cost. Photos available.

Mark Ewert

DIPTYCH: ALLEN GINSBERG, WILLIAM BURROUGHS

Gemini	Aquarius
Jewish	W.A.S.P.
62	75
blowjobs	dry-humping
none; acid in freezer	booze, pot, methadone (?)
New York—new apartment—	Kansas—lakeside cabin—
bidet	rowboat
"I have no secrets—tell	"I have nothing and no one
everything!"	to betray."
stewed apples, fishy	fried eggs, toaster-
rice gruel, flaky	hashbrowns, orange
Italian pastries from	juice, sourdough toast,
Vesuvio's	Lipton's tea with milk
	and sugar
palsy, one side of face	half of one pinky missing
The Co-Evolutionary	Soldier of Fortune and
Quarterly and Fairness,	The Shaman's Drum,
Accuracy in	coffee table
Reporting, bathroom	
secret Tantric lectures,	The Necronomicon, spare
bedroom	bedroom
purple and gold lapel pin,	wristwatch with hologram of
American Academy	cat's head
of Arts and Letters	
Shaivite trident, kitchen	too many to list fully:
	blowgun and blackjack,
	living room; club "to
	drive off wild dogs,"
	back door; loaded gun,
	in bed (!); fully
	operational, pinky-sized
	pistol, file cabinet...
circa age 12: mother went	circa age 10: was detested by
crazy, frightening him;	the "proper" friends
the sheathes around	of his parents, one of
her nerves were	whom said that he had
disintegrating	"the look of a sheep-
	killing dog"
never performed live with Beck	never saw an alien
mentholated skin balm	pot and cigarette smoke

THE MECHANISM

Jump off the merry-go-round
whose jangling roar and varnished glare
jolt you awake

Veer out of the path of those plunging
creatures with flaring scarlet nostrils
vacant insect gaze

The whirling sheets of printed paper
rhetoric and propaganda
blown into your face

A desecrated dream-world, gone
from pastoral to derelict
to post-disaster waste

Then force yourself back on and seize
the lever of the mechanism.
Now hard-brake.

BEETLE

In the sealed gap between the inner and outer
window (neither of which can be opened)
of the downstairs cloakroom—a large dark beetle.

For a long time I watched this investigation
of its prison's limits, the effort to climb
the thin leaded edge of the bar dividing
the outer window into smaller panes.

But impossible to get a purchase on
glass or metal: after each effort, straining
upward a few inches, it topples backwards.

At last, after the six thin jointed legs
had flailed, bicycling helplessly, like the limbs
of bodies falling through space, somehow
it rights itself and struggles back to its feet.

There is a pause, as if mustering strength,
a posture of tenacity, what seems a stare
of stubborn hope. Then the process starts again.

I do not want to monitor its death.
But unless I break the window, I cannot
release it or myself. Then the beetle-god
blesses us both; next morning, the space is empty.

Lawrence Ferlinghetti

ARE THERE NOT STILL FIREFLIES

Are there not still fireflies
                              in America
Are there not still four-leaf clovers
Is not our land still beautiful
          our fields not full of armed enemies
              our cities never bombed to oblivion
                                        by foreign invaders
                    never occupied by iron armies
                                    speaking iron tongues
Are not our warriors still valiant
                                    ready to defend us
Are not our senators
                        still wearing fine togas
Are we not still a great people
              in the greatest country in all the world

Is this not still a free country

Are not our fields still ours
                our gardens still full of flowers
                            our ships with full cargoes

Why then do some still fear
            the barbarians are coming
                            coming coming
                                    in their huddled masses
        (What is that sound that fills the ear
                            drumming drumming?)

Is not Rome still Rome
Is not Los Angeles still Los Angeles
Is not beauty still beauty
And truth still truth
Are there not still poets
Are there not still lovers
Are there not still mothers

                  sisters and brothers

Is there not still a full moon

                once a month

Are there not still fireflies
Are there not still stars at night
Can we not still see them

            in bowl of night

                signalling to us our manifest destinies

Lawrence Ferlinghetti

FOR THE SILENT MAJORITY

And a vast paranoia sweeps across the land
And America turns the attack on its Twin Towers
Into the beginning of the Third World War
The war with the Third World

And the terrorists in Washington
Are drafting all the young men

And no one speaks

And they are rousting out
All the ones with turbans
And they are flushing out
All the strange immigrants

And they are shipping all the young men
To the killing fields again

And no one speaks

And when they come to round up
All the great writers and poets and painters
The National Endowment of the Arts of Complacency
Will not speak

While all the young men
Will be killing all the young men
In the killing fields again

So now is the time for you to speak
All you lovers of liberty
All you lovers of the pursuit of happiness
All you lovers and sleepers
Deep in your private dream

While they are killing all the young men

Now is the time for you to speak
O silent majority
Before they come for you

2/12/03

AIR STRIKES: 1999

The owl ate her chicks.
All her chicks. She gazes
owl-like from her perch as if
all owls everywhere
not just the ones in the Belgrade zoo
eat their chicks.

A cat on the stones a continent away
charges every passerby
who crosses her perimeter—
claws, bites, her scrawny body
hurled like a cluster bomb
at every passing leg—
her newborn wriggling blind
at the center of her range.

Serb children no longer believe
in holiday fireworks. Serb babies
cringe at a lullaby. Serb soldiers shoot.
Kill, wound, burn. Their
babies wail and die.
The Bengal tiger in the Belgrade zoo
has gnawed off its own back feet.

Allen Ginsberg

LINES FOR CREELEY'S EAR

The whole
weight of
everything
too much

my heart in
the subway
pounding
subtly

headache
from smoking
dizzy
a moment

riding
uptown to see
Karmapa
Buddha tonite.

Dec 13, 1976

LINES FOR CREELEY'S EAR

The whole
weight of
everything
too much

my heart in
the subway
pounding
subtly

head ache
from smoking
dizzy
a moment

riding
uptown to see
Karmapa
Buddha tonite.

Dec 13, 1976

Allen Ginsberg

Sara Goodman

THE URGE TO DESTROY IS A CREATIVE URGE

It is finally finished
My village on the floor
Red Ferraris and white pick-up trucks
Picking up hitch hikers
Red light Green light
The yellow light is missing
But nobody misses it
I don't even have to ask the village
I hear their buzz

I came home late tonight
I stumbled over something
The overpass crumbled
Into gray plastic chunks
A woman cried like a wolf with a fork stabbed in her eye
But she feels so far away, I will not sob this time
Only let one eyeball drip
For a tender moment
And pray for her, a silent continent

All this before I tuck myself in
The blanket stitched red and blue,
Yellow at the trim.
I wake up at 4 am to the barrel of my gun,
Shaped in the form of a rapid eye,
Caught in the web of my dream catcher
The people in the village have decided it would be fun
If they throw a parade
Over the crushed woman's grave

Thich Nhat Hanh

SILENCE

The paper smells wonderful
as I turn the pages of this ancient book.
The water in my glass
smiles to me with crystal eyes.
Suddenly oceanic waves come up one after another
with their foamy heads.
A cold stone
summons the fog
up on the distant mountain
where the wind is howling hard.

I wake up.
The tip of my tongue is frozen
by the dewdrops
that have been sent to me
by a blade of grass on a late night.
Light flashes across
like the blade of a sword.
Perhaps it is the beginning of a storm.
Clouds rise very quickly.
From the East, urgently,
the sound of the horns is calling.

Where is my palm-leaf raincoat of years ago?
The winds are chasing after the leaves.
The lines and strokes
your brush used to trace
are brown,
the color of your arm,
the sweat that penetrates the rice field.

In this moment, our planet is lost
somewhere in the unknown,
and the giant bird
is shaking its wings in outer space.
Space in puddles
is splashing.
Space is exploding.

There is a sun
struggling up and down
in the ocean
like a giant fish with enormous red eyes.
My telephoto lens
is trying to catch the images of prehistory.
Look! The door is just unlocked,
and the future is let free.
For many lives,
that door has prevented the future from fleeing.

This morning on my way to the woods,
through the singing of the bird,
I know you are there, free,
free on a green path.
There are buds, flowers, and tiny leaves
waving to space.
The hand,
the hand that holds the baton of the talented artist
conducts the world of sound.
All sounds return
to this one point
of great silence,
this point
of great emptiness.

There is too much light—
too much light for a baby just entering life.
I see now
our grandmother
with her hair tied behind her head
in the form of an onion.
She is sweeping bamboo leaves.
She begins to gather the leaves into a pile
and burn them.
The smoke is rising,
warming up the sky.
The Buddha smiles behind a thin cloud.
Tonight the moon is full.

Alamgir Hashmi

POST SCROTUM
In Memoriam Samuel Beckett

Watt? Yes. But the same when the Mal'oun died
in the island; this island severed,
repoussé, reeling with peat-reek;
this drizzle of grief—
interminable falling on the wide sea.
Moll's face saffron-coloured, hair like
petals plucked from a white chrysanthemum;
local boys on stout or busy at hurling;
and our scriveners, on regular beat up in London,
aping accents of the English gentry.
I broadcast in Irish then, from Radio Éireann,
the right embers and all that fall to the ashes
or whatever I often whispered to myself
through Murphy, Philips, or Grundig.
No, not Grundig, for the word grounds the air,
the mind slips out of form in that language,
is not hand in glove as now. Example:
with a handschuh your hands feel they wear shoes;
the foot's in the mouth; and you write with your feet.
Paris is O. K. Paris is all right. Paris is O. K. All right.
I was lecteur d'anglais in that place, teaching Doublin'
English and writing like Thom A. Becket what no one,
except J. J. in some arseholy state or other, would attempt—
in a language of my own.
I hear now that across the Chunnel
one side tells the other it's French I wrote;
the other side calls it English, or by other appellatives;
such as would divide the protestant cake in catholic portions
and make for a nice debate
in the Parliament of European Foules.

If I said Parnell was no string-pulling
politician, women would be tightening the girth
of their drawers with double-knotted strings.
I left because truelove had run out of the vein,
the earth turning no end but negative;
its slow poisons free a sweet violet in my lungs.
And, yes, French had a point or two.
That dusty potato dropped in 1921 or 1845,
it named the apple of the earth—
to say nothing of the rotten core.
Peeling. Peeling.

"NAVAJO RELIGION"

The holy chance. Isn't it just. Some people say just go with the next thing, don't look back, and those people interest me. The hoop transformation. Don't we ever! We're in the hoop now, don't you know. Knots and tangles. Attraction of good may be one part of it, but also attraction of bad. I have your number. A cement floor you said. And then your wife sending you an e-mail. *Sending you an e-mail?* Think about it. What we did was a whole lot different from that. Where the night is spent.

He runs on the water. All of you run the first night, then you come back. You get scared, the red flag, but then the object like the Towering Inferno. You said it: It's not rational. Did you notice that you've become the you? I held two of you in my arms last night, but that's as it should be. Might be. When changing woman. Get scared and come back. I've learned how to wait, but I'm not waiting. I'm busy.

Ashes blowing. But let's not go there yet. Night three? Another place not yet here. Where was I? Holding bow and arrow. That's the image. But he's never called the hunter, is he? It's all so playful. Playful my foot. Humping themselves up in the middle. That guy sticking his fingers up under my skirt last night in the métro. What did he know about it? I gave him a sharp jab with my elbow.

Lyn Hejinian

from THE FATALIST

The goose is gone and the goose girl with it
in the erotically tormented tale whose hero carries a map
of the areas most effected and that includes your neighborhood.
A sense of doom hangs over everything. I too in retrospect
far less ominous once lost my faith in art and stood with small numbers
of good people in protest. No one paid any attention
but I did. One creates out of love and gives art
as a gift. I don't regard this as a flashback
in the sense that you mean it (i.e., as drug-induced).
What you express is a sense of disorientation, a sense
of desperate disgust. "I'm fucked up" is a self-accusation. I too
am an asshole. But you have to be cheerful to be oblivious
and there must be something in the pitch of sorry questions.
At least we are willing to entertain this possibility with incredulity
but there is logic to it too. We have both been using logic
just to be sure. Still, the phrase "fear maintains"
is a little fuzzy. Clings with a hard-c sound to go
with the words constant and clipped link fear more closely
to the fingernails—the sense of being scratched. He points
to some guy, she points to some woman, it can point to nothing
at all (in which case it is ghostly) or to something
that hasn't yet appeared (in which case it is clairvoyant)
even though I'm not sure you were conscious of it, but—
well, let's just say that it was conscious of you, the setting
overhung with live oak trees. In the distance fog clings to the horizon
looking down onto the stage. Someone expressed fear. The guy
grabbed the egg. But is it just simple contact that we want?
As the planes took off we all noted the singing ("Mine eyes have seen
the coming," etc.), a copy (they say "it offers enormous clarity") of which
brings "closure"—a fundamental right—to—you?

66

Subtraction is the assassin's game (or gain). Outright war
requires divisions. Without the self-righteousness of a cavalry man
or prowess of the athlete whose jersey bears a prime number I am xeroxing
onward toward a state that will be called gloomily critical
and destroyed but first there is the dreamy mixing, then the muscular
kneading, then the aggressive punching down and barking
through the open window and the fog follows the pale sunlight and the white dog
that have become regular features in Gertrude Stein's *Wars*
I Have Seen. Bread means what?—that one's antecedents weren't nomadic? Where
shall I put the roses and how? What would Freud say? You say
that the failure of "the American left" to understand
"the American people's visceral need for revenge" is "inhuman."
Are the three depressed youths on skateboards simply hanging out
of context? Where we (drifting past the female stars) are today (trespassing
on a private beach) is where we have been
though things are never the same
from one moment to the next in the context now
of an unavoidable awareness of a terrible situation
that mythologized itself as utopian from the very start. Consider
the utopian dissidents who founded communities as kernels
from which a better belief in the existence
(and, for some, presence) of paradise would grow. I have no idea at all
what the budget is. The psychic economy is wild
and won't accumulate and stabilize. Isn't that what Freud would say? Imagine
preparing! Where are you getting your materials? It is easy to surrender
them, hard to win them back.

———

The dot arrives abruptly. Between words
there are swimmers swimming in a dashing sea—(the sort
of thing that adolescents achieve). And yet things must begin
at some point so why not with a dot inevitably? This one
includes a shell-studded opalescent kitchenette
but is otherwise generic. How much better is the dot
in Paul Klee's notebooks! His dot has no terminus!
It has duration. Mine is apparently recursive.
This will now have to be checked. I need a bigger envelope
and a stronger case if I'm going to engage with the literature
that music provides. Anything that goes into an airplane
must meet the same regulations as those dictating what goes
into a mailbox. Pedalling underlies everything. Time,
which we've received and mostly cherished, inhabits
the questions. These are not negative spaces
toward which we bound, strong and specific. What tenuous attachments
these speculative yearnings are that bind us
to all that we care about. They need not be at odds with each
other as well as with the sense that we should be doing something—
something more? something else? I can't allow myself
to be distracted by poignant crises since I want to keep up
without risk of harassment or punishment
and if this will require a special session I urge
that it be called frequently. I'd like that
very much. We'll set our trap for judges and find them
sitting in blame. That will produce more
and better confusion. It comes in the middle
of the night accompanied by fever and trembling. I vomit
and lose one day.

———

Another transition is underway in all directions. It's not much like
the one from night to unearthed or from everyman
to fund-raising. Still, it offers a promise of something I had hoped
someone would discern but without the bathos
that the sharing of it would provoke. We need velocity
to enter reality. We nod, knowing we nod with knowledge
because of the bumps, jostled
at a point of maximal excitement in the adventure
of our ongoing collaboration by the insights
we cannot communicate to each other. I want to explain
why "the patience of the gray pony bearing the fat weeping man" means
nothing but I can't even stand corrected, which is the same thing
and altogether different, and at the end of the story (I despise
military terminology) you will find me in bed
when you get there so that I can wake up. There's still no end
in sight. Do remember when D had the idea
of disguising her real identity and passing herself
off as a licensed detective? Strange
physiological adventures are going on everyday unseen.

Amy Hollowell

MONDAY MORNING IS ON THE RUN

What's in the air cannot be undone
A spring breeze coolly not bringing snow
No salt or sand dune
In the scrubby garden out back
Early, a sun bath
The first time and as ever
Each time and as ever
Within innumerable landscapes of here
Now unfolding
As always
And here remains free
The moment still at large and promising
Nothing definitive
Swift vehicles in transit descend the sloping avenue
Unseen white roses lie ready in their beds
Cries from near scaffolding pierce and grind
A blackbird call
A backdoor slam
A murmur of young fir trees bending
Their frail shadows gain without gain
Wind has no appointment
It blows
Brown hair whips, Herald Tribune flaps, then a fluttering fall to rest
Arising
Real time is not gone nor arriving
Never coming soon
Never trimmed, never lacking
At this low wicker table
All is flush
Space being actual and beyond
In the bright morning
Words are like fingers
Pointing at the sky

KILLED

It happened on a small street in a big city and
         was a mixture of what to expect in a big city
                 and what never happens on a small street.
                   I think of the tenants directly across on
                 the same floor with their shades drawn for
         the eight weeks before the bulb died. Blood
smeared on the glass pane, soaking the bed
         where he'd lain. I'd never before thought of
                 that detail to crime scenes where even the
                         flicking of a light switch or drawing of a
                 shade is disruptive. I think of the man's smile
         when our dogs met in the street—two retrievers
like comedians. But only after he'd been stabbed
         repeatedly by a released mental patient he'd
                 picked up at a bar did I find out his name from
                         others, his occupation from the paper, that
                 he'd just got his big break with a photograph
         of Freedy Johnston for Interview, though he
wasn't happy and was cruising a lot. Homicide
         detectives collected in front of the brownstone
                 like an episode of Law & Order, yet someone
                         helped me know who died by saying the dog's
                 name. Dorothy, a yellow lab mix, was seen
         pacing and whining in the stairwell by a down-
stairs neighbor who released her onto the street,
         where she must have felt frantic and duped when
                 she saw him walking away. She paced back and
                         forth in front of the stoop until the afternoon when
                 a woman who knew the man and the dog spotted her.

His friend said she felt uneasy, then, getting one of
her own dog's leashes for Dorothy, because she
        knew Richard would never let his dog loose.
            Sometimes, she looked after Dorothy for a
                weekend, so with her key, went into the
                building, up the stairs, and saw the door ajar.
        She didn't want this. They caught the pick-up,
who'd left his wallet at the crime scene and
        stolen Richard's camera to pawn for drugs.
            There was a fight. Probably, Richard woke up
                to see him stealing, but the pick-up took a
                cleaver on the same night that O.J. allegedly
        knifed two citizens, and multiply stabbed him.
The detectives also know that the man
        whose big break photograph would be
            out in a month did not die, immediately,
                a notion they drummed into the ears of
                the feckless young man from the floor
        below who'd heard a terrible fight and
seen from the window a strange man
        exit in a bloody shirt at dawn, then
            released Dorothy and gone to work.
                I think of my own well-meaning golden
                retriever who is eager to warn me of a
        stranger's approach. But that is the
terminal of his guard capacity.
        After that, he stands back ready to
            greet or melt to the floor and I think of
                Dorothy, hunched and still, licking out of
                love for any salt of her Richard's body,
        the blood that layered his skin until
the pick-up left the door awake.

SHREDDED PEACE

There's No Big Message except hope you've had a good time
While listening to this

While somewhere the Great Novel is being shredded
And I get to stand up and say my piece
Or at least a piece of my piece
"Shredded Peace: Anti-War Poem"

I will never sit in that class again, a stone
Eating away at the heart of existence

Plenty of homeless people want to read my poems
They are lucky I stand at the newsstand
Cursing the politicians and making faces

Maybe all I'm saying is it's a real job
Being unemployed

D. J. Huppatz

APOETICS

flickering frame blink

           a searching lure

                        detached eyes

                                    grant limits

The voice-chant in a rhythmic pattern. Try to make sense of it. Rewind. Analyse its frequencies, break down the waves into ones and not-ones, see if they still foam...

Where can we meet in this excess of light?

                                    ((a textus?))

                                    :an open hole:

microtonal impulses in a binary mode rush --interrupt-- *was the migration of the larynx a technological breakthrough or part of the process of built-in obsolescence?*

                      crosshairs quivering

                      with excitement

eat chips with coke-tongue numbness
your finger twitches
unwondering addictedly to hollow hallucinations the means of perception lost & body colonized with sensations slipped quickly through the doors of Victory Mansions unnoticed (or so thought)

                —let's play the lugubrious game—

                        how much is a toxic dose of writing?

                        <UNDO>

...sensations flowing through inert bodies moulded into a terminal machine. Now take flight, that the vibrations of your wings may jam the starter motor of a bulldozer in the Brazilian rainforests.

John Coltrane taking Julie Andrews for a waltz or
Jack Spicer a radio picking up messages from Mars
or Derrida's sphincter...

They shot Andy Warhol, she said.
(this is how the dead write to the dead)
Then:
An old military-looking gentleman appeared, with a frightfully severe face, a pack of native servants, and a boy and a girl; it was a jolly thrilling party, and we felt more than a bit keen to know more of them. *Culture forsooth! Albert, get my gun...*

Be the transistor that created me.
Horse have two eye. No eye, no can see. No can see, no can go. See?
A verb, scentless attractor, needs to be plugged in. Gentle reader, put your finger here, feel how wet and warm...

>> switch on automatic obedience to smart technology >>
[Eichmann, the technician: "I dunno me. Only work here."]

...those are not mountains that you see, nor sky nor grass nor clouds nor trees but the landscape that dreamed me.

I Hassan i Sabbah rub out the word forever:
NO MORE PAPPA-MAMMA

(after giggle & scream, woof woof

Michael Huxley

ALL FOR FUTURE REFERENCE

In slowing my vehicle past the construction zone,
how many times have I recreated Him
slaving hotter than sin, beneath a sweaty sky ablaze,
for submission to the porno palace?
Invocated His always consensual presence
in moments of self-gratification?
At such times (as driving by), I would gladly forgo my future
to hear the timbre of His spoken, baritone affirmative.

But do not break the spell
by giving voice to your opinions,
save to extol praise of my reflection in your eyes,
approbation of how my playing you,
how my freshly shaven cheek,
drawn against your beard stubble
        evokes an undying response.

Allow the shadow my head casts upon your excellent face,
as we lean into the preliminary tongue-swirl,
to supersede, eclipse your belief system.
Neither before nor after we pull them over our heads,
        do not present a worldview
as gravity compels our tank tops to the ground.
You may introduce your name, Priapus,
you may celebrate the boldness of my gesture
        as I disengage your fly,
        as I rise to the occasion
of your scent, your taste, your touch.
But do not presume that I will care to know you further.

You and I amount to
an aggregate of tissue and blood in motion,
swells and curves of pectoral and glutei,
        a heft of scrotum,
a vein of carnality mined from navel to anus,
from tongue-in-mouth to response,
party to no familial dynamic or politic,
screaming jolts, bucking bolts of semen at best.
Pressed against, into one another,
we are proof that glory is found in the seeking,

in failing to draw as close to retribution in coming
        as we desire.
Equate our abandon with the spiritual, should you see fit,
        but keep it to yourself
as we reassemble our separate identities post-ejecta,
as we smooth the t-tops once again
        down our exaggerated torsos.

I do not care to hear your position on the war,
        who your heroes are,
that you prefer reading to watching television,
that you favor foreign film.
Perhaps it would matter were I available,
        if you existed,
but even so, that would still depend.
Point taken, is it not gratifying enough
to observe how marvelously sculpted
you exist in my farewell sunglasses,
that I will hold you in my highest estimation
until the day of my last self-involvement,
until my fantastical, testicular Rolodex
is incinerated into cremains?

But of course you proved homosexual, enamored of me.
In coupling, as in pornographic depictions of love,
        everything clicked.
        Effortlessly shifting gears
from one tangible of body worship to another,
you moved me, Baby, have moved me before
and will time and again, well as it should be.

I, perhaps your greatest fear,
am watching you grind your smoke
        beneath your booted heel
into the dirt that constitutes you.
Watching you scale, with pie-in-the-sky resignation,
the I-beam of your pre-occupational hazard,
        watching,
up-shifting into third and then fourth,
        watching
as you diminish in the geographic distance,
I have cataloged and filed you,
my oblivious, (no doubt) hetero hero,
        all for future reference.

Fred Johnston

CIRCLE DANCE

First time like understanding water, the skin of water in bright light, turning makes poetry, each line a muscle, stanzas rippling out like language assembled; this, with sealight churning on a white plaster ceiling, chairs squeaking, no looking elsewhere; how a girl could do this, stockinged on the planked floor, by a turn of hand a word formed, the graceless day rearranged, sun on the brass of a door, the ropes of the sea gathering up against the harbour; first time to catch in her open eye the Fish of Utterance, Salmon of Speech, say what you like, this is witchery, floor a heath; at the threshold, stone Colonial staircase in rain up into the lofts of splendid houses, B&B windows fogged in early fretting breaths, doors sad unknocked; where the great ships berthed now a silence, beckoning away and she dancing still against high flamboyant windows, dead fingers on the desks, we could go now but no, she flails with lovely energy in the white neon; body moulds itself into the putty air, children fidget; is this what it is to dance? Call the poem out—priests ribboned for exorcism; have it roar in the shape of her, quiver in her or under the skin of her; imagine tracing with a permitted finger the soft moist loops and whorls, stain the half-moon face radiant with allowance; what of taxis and unused 'phone kiosks and chip shops larded with pulp-thick air; what of the young men cross-footed, already fat-arsed in their pissory, hungry here? To breathe her, bending the knee; with two hands ends the turn, back to her seat, solemn in applause, The Baptist's head in her hands; have you not thought, no, imagined, the blushing neck of her against your open mouth at the last moment, making you make language? And the damaged sea in a window of old glass, and white painted frames; and flowers in vases for greeting, and her going away?

nikki d. KATHERINE

FAITH RENEWED

In the icy dark of September's despair with a doubting heart
I timidly crept to the most distant corner of the garden and buried the bulbs

Today, suddenly golden heads push through cool damp earth
singing spring, shouting hope, shining warmth
my soul soars
such a glorious February morning
sunshine paints a smile upon my lips
my laughter full of joy!
I remember not, why last fall
I was so forlorn

Eliot Katz

GREGORY'S LAST LINES

He was a poet of silk and the shredding of silk.
No earthling nor deity remained immune from his probing questions.
When the academy turned its head for a pulitzer second
he slipped an enlightened humor worm into the gut of poetry
    that hasn't yet wriggled its way out.
With fountain pen tears he mourned the nationalism of the nation
    even as he hosannahed the home run.
He fooled death, coaxing it into the soup of life
    every time but for one.

Writing in "Many Have Fallen" about American soldiers
    marched by Army into radioactive bomb blasts
Gregory wrote: "All survived / ...until two decades later
when the dead finally died"—
a last line of stunning poetry enough to make the top
    of Emily D's head pop off.

In 1983, Andy Clausen brought him to carouse
    our New Brunswick bars.
We stopped first at my kitchen table electric typewriter,
    where Gregory pulled his pocket notebook
and tapped out a piece for *Long Shot* magazine.
The poem was called "Delacroix Mural at St. Sulpice".
Deep into typing, Gregory stopped & asked
    what thought I of his last three pencil'd lines.
I eyed his notebook, said I liked 'em but not as much
    as the rest of the poem.
I thought he might write three new ones on the spot—
but instead he stood up, waved his left hand suavely
& declared the poem done at what'd been
    the fourth-to-last line:
"I know the ways of god / by god!"
He knew how to end / at the ending.

I had the chance to read him "Ode to the West Wind"
     on his cancer bed:
"If Winter comes, can Spring be far behind?"
After approaching mortality's last breath in summer,
     he arose to see another new year.
Now, I hear his ashes will be buried in Rome's cemetery,
a neighbor of Shelley & the one whose name is writ in water.
In "Getting to the Poem", Gregory ended:
"I will live / and never know my death."
Who can say whether he was aware of that golden moment
     when the breath says "no"?—
but he damn sure got to the poems.

Death, Gregory knew your secret name,
he knew your habits, your weapons, your games—
now give his verse the life it deserves
     & do what you will with his gilgamesh hair.

John Kinsella

BEGINNING WITH FIRST AND LAST LINES FROM EDWIN DENBY: A SET DESIGN

"Are the lozenges projected from the square of these views.)"
Offset and rounded, scuff marks, and

accumulations, cauterized as friendship
Rejigged, just happened by, coincidence, chance;
in our despairing we looked out beyond
mail slots in doors, castigations, sacrebleu,

old chum, cobber, mate, buddy; mise en scène
you hide behind, out there, the nature;
wooden fences, pickets, are what's

remembered, the crossbars on which side,
the terrors of fences backing
on to laneways—not in your suburb,

edging effects, for metaphor is not undead here,
but is placement is luxury
goods;)

"In an inch of forest violets are found"
a pocket of air packed with sound,
mortar and lime, plumb-bob line,

pre-fab, modular, don't think about
the sound of the word/s, tomorrowed city

gardens, Cartesian stuff, ELEGANT,
infernal retina, optically machine

Le Corbusier, the wavy setting,
that postcard from Barcelona, a city I quite like

despite a scarcity of vegan
cookery, but that's personal,
fourth person figurative.

"Each is a private addict of love."
scrunched in front of the télé;

                                   going there
doesn't protect you
from the movies,
which is where you are, without nouns,
trend, or destiny: these guides we read;

a word from a glossy: "cinemarchitectural",
after the main course, directorships.

"Three old sheepherders so filthy in their ways"
drink piss on the shotholed verandah,
their camera-eyes reaching through forest
not far off, a broken fence where sheep
move through, breaking
summer shortage, a dialectic, unhistory,
no new layers, the canopy depth-planed further,
either way, a shorter forest history.

"Here where a blank sky puts me at the center"
I move suddenly away, this house a cloister,
a company register; up north,

Karratha—say—owned by the company,
cyclone screens in front of glass,
air-conditioning pumping all year 'round;

these are porno and dieting towns.
observation is its own bigotry.

tides drop metres,
mud-crabs filter effluent,
digitalized mangroves. community,
breaking bread, the conversation of friends.

"When after hearing last, I fell asleep"
to rejoin the speech, good kitchen products
global not local,

    this industry
that leisures time, a basic instruction english,
lower-cased, at hand, clawed.

"The street is where people meet according to law"
and imagery, a choice of rough carpet, cordage,
thick walls; this is not prêt-à-porter;

       they wired
the houses wrongly and law suits
blossom unlike precedent, and they set

nothing: to think, we loved in the brief space
between shed and fence, as if psychologically
it could be called love, it's just therapy.

"Love has not stopped, has not started by fucking."
but we try it anyway, our disconnected bodies
having a say of sorts, scattered, eulogizing,
plumbing]

    all household appliance
based on sex-slavery, the ads

say we took a holiday, in the Alps,
or locally, a shack by the beach;
a chalet, self-contained,
mostly insulated.

Near seabirds.

"On fancy fronts of houses but strong"
numbering, as here he was, one five two,
ordering not lost, path-cracks and backs
and those concrete boats on river
not sinking, the field about: subdivided,
the quarter acre, Ken's apartment
in Brooklyn, which was a score: lucky.
Or cultured up, the Ainslie Roberts—
dark curlew—on the wall;
drinking Cointreau off glass tables,
and learning about Passover, as if
in the house we might be there.

"A desert is fine for engineering"
and decorative roofs, as if all for praying;

what room for free will, sandblower
and tinted goggles, sets of epics

but not blank verse—these words
are taken from a sonnet, a deception,

a ruse of snakes and waterholes,
briefly cured, like King O'Malley.

"A beauty of doubt that is homeless and not brief"
parks and fructates, semi-apocalyptic,
sequencing big rooms and vestibules,

we obsess over the feature window,

leadlight, describe a kookaburra
where a woodpecker might be,
as if you'd written

what crossed your mind
in the back room: you went there
for the light and only.

"Neighbor sneaks refuse to my roof"
or listen through sinkholes and drains;
central heating, the Chrysler buildings house-style,

upkept, expensive; conferring
in rooms, translation and forum

etiquette, this resonating-less language,
this homely imprisonment, ballistic
economics;

"Sunday on the senator's estate"
phone cards and fiscal restraint
those Cuban episodes: we all want to lunch
with Castro, diasporically,
ah, Miami.

"Recall that events are roomy"
and our characters small…

"All we survivors within float"
where schools banish Spanish,
enforce English,

language

identity

policy: seated speaker inscribes mimesis.
translationese.

calque.

THE HORIZONTAL EGO-PLAYING MACHINE

On the map
And curve around

Bend lap
Divisions defined

And so defended
With efforts to

**

Assert alas
Elastically

And what seeming
To rival

Let pause
By comparison

**

(In minuscule patterns
Of urges and

Degrees...)

**

For instance, if the wind
Bleeds into

Instances rolling back
Along the type-hills

Mimetic and structured
Like an event

The called semantics
Of syntax intact

And cracked jaw of
Comparisons

Of matters
Practiced but impractical

Chaotic motion tempered
By the distended constant

**

Or the uneven blanks
The window travels

Across the viable registers
It lances

Original echoes
And advances advice

For revising
Even if this wisdom

Repeats itself you're not
Obligated to attend

To it though certainly we
Would appreciate your

Prescience
I can scarcely cite that

Down before it's
Evaporated, friends

My lyric's been
Creeping all day

Into the vanished—
Engines

AMIRI

Imagine being compared with Michel Foucault. Not today

but there you are standing at the edge of the curb
40 years back waiting for the light to change,
jaywalkin the blues in the roar of ghostly traffic
"a constant trembling rain" and the El screeching overhead
     at the rushhour
Screen ratio 2:35 to 1 and totally grainy
and autumn has ended in con-tro-versy.

I—I just don't get it. The sun arks its way into fragments
and the life of a shadow suddenly veers off
and Satie was flooding the air
and the neon begins consuming the darkness

Who's going to verify this?
Who's going to plunge down the rabbit hole?
I hear the cooing of pigeons on the sill.
I hear the typewriter typing
the phone ringing. All this fuss over nothing.
Dead cigarettes singing.

There's no wave crashing the shore.
The trolley tracks are paved over. Metaphors
are banished. There's nothing
inside the bubble. Nothing
matters. Nothing
is next. The one building number 27 scratched on the door—
Cooper Square becomes folklore.
A scattering of leaves cover the cobblestones,
frayed at the edges.

Speckled sunlight disappears, reappears
in rapid succession.

"Those
were
clouds
silly!"

A ball bounces into the gutter.

But for some reason the photograph had never been taken,

or another dream leaves you empty.

This isn't the way it happens.
This isn't the right time of day
This isn't the Cedar Bar even

so Times Square has changed
and the grungy backyards of Newark
and the plumbing is rusty. So?

Parts of ourselves come into existence
with each brief encounter. Parts of us exit.

For that one brief instant the shadow
becomes invisible as it crosses the street
and the pages keep turning over.

POEM
*"The color of stepped on gum
is the color of our times."*
—Tom Clark

Sooty blue laced with clinker grey
muck brown streaked with dirty pink
sticking nastily to a sole.

The lighting of our times is strip or strobe.
God's in his heaven playing with a macro-chip.

Acid rain is the weather of our times.
Acrid cities smoke like spit-sogged cigars.

The homeless bed down with a blanket of pollution.
Shooting up is not a Western.

Tasteless junk food is the shape of our times.
Excess and obesity prevail.

Rapfunk and screams are the tunes of our times
percussing to the rhythm of bombs.

TV and opinion polls
are substitutes for thinking:
we fully support, or somewhat, not at all.

Pansy Maurer-Alvarez

AFTER WATCHING *SCRATCHING THE INNER FIELDS*
a piece choreographed by Wim Vandekeybus
performed at the Théâtre des Abbesses
Paris, March 2001

I feel great sunny morning   open window   breathe in   get out in it

Stuff the clouds in your pocket   but Oklahoma City

Documentary keeps staying in my mind   Wind and it's hot with

Rain requiem forming   tension mounting and wind goes black sky

Tornado warnings go out   WE HAVE TORNADO ON THE GROUND

TORNADO   ON   THE   GROUND

NO time place   to go but stay home in the shelter

          "Jump into the bathtub for your life!"

Sunshine after tornado   mother and daughter walk

Through living room wreckage   they can't understand   lost everything

Discover China figurine   undamaged   not theirs

          Between the storms it is impossible
          to stay inside the body's too fragile
          to smell me like jasmine   taste
          me like pepper   lick my eyes
          before the end of the world gets here
          is another way of saying

WORD OUT OF INTERIOR

Newborn baby downstairs cries like a machine, has now
cried herself out, might just whimper a while
Suddenly I desire interior images   out of the cave: slap of the language
first scream   of need or danger   first rough rub on tongue
      Breathe   Feel words entering mouth from way back dark

                          Last night I watched
7 women move into metal light of cold requiem dance
in wondrous night of their voyages: rain   earth   blood
          across their inner fields they sighed

Touch me like sand with your hands of metal
see me with tongue
Hear me slowly   carefully know why (speak)
you might be going

Michael McClure

EAGLE EVOLUTIONS
with a little help from my friends
Hans Peeters and Sterling Bunnell

... AND NOW I FIND THAT THERE ARE THREE LINES THROUGH THE EAGLES
(THESE BIRDS LIKE POETRY HAVE MANY SOURCES!) 1. The Bald Eagle
is Fish Eagle like the one on the coast of Kenya
that wrote his white crest on my eyes as I floated
in rain-flecked waves. 2. The Golden Eagle, dark brown, ochre brown,
ragged and powerful outline, deep-staring eyes, comes through
another tribe, from the Buteo Hawks and is related
to the Red Tail hovering over Twin Peaks
and the Park nearby. 3. The Monkey Eagles, Crowned Eagles,
are related to the Cooper Hawk, Goshawks, Sharp Shins,
from the Accipiter line.   AND

THEY

ARE
ALL

EAGLES

(and
spirits)

and they move me
deeply

as they roar in my sleep
and in the day land

with mottled primaries as delicate as cliffs
and vanes fine as the milky breasts of chinchillas.

94

CANYON CAMEO
for Hans and Pam

ON THE BLUE-GRAY AND GLINTING CLIFF-FACE WALL
a tiny bag of spider silk is hung,
all velveted to gray with sluff
that's shed from rocks and oaks above.
Resting on a twig beside the web
is an iridescent wing—green, blue, purple,
silver, gold. The air is light
with sage and tarweed scent.
The nearby pond sends gleams
of summer sun—but broken up
by noses of the frogs
and turtles' beaks. The garter
snake that's resting there
IS
PLEASED
to
be.
The soaring eagle dips
to earth
as free
as thought.

Exhibit A: Your animal instincts
Exhibit B: Civilized death

Replace your vision
Remove eyes & insert fiber optics
all this light & music
universal x-ray variation
likened to a melody
see its   over there   & in here   in you
blackholes' enormous gravity
battles enormous opportunity to destroy self
look into sun
cornea damage makes vision more interesting

Time's hamfisted sensibilities
tops list of worst invention yet
see its   reflection here   & over there

bad timing is everything
you can configure games & master dealmaking
or hold hands & make a circle
you decide

beware of bogeyman burn out
of night lights   dying suns   & messiahs
there are bound to be regrets
when last words are to yr killer

Sylvia Miles

FAREWELL MY DEAR FRIEND

'Tis true that many will miss you
Though I hope not more than me.
For 'twas often said in jest at a
Fête or function we'd be there
      for all to see
You, with your unique and spiffy look
And humor ever intact
I, with fingerless gloves and leopard hat.
Indeed, that was a photo 'op' in fact.
Yes, you lived your life
      facing endless strife,
All with grace and great aplomb.
Never bitter, just the witty and
      clever dry wry Crisp.
Proving in fact, dear Quentin, that
   one should not go back to
      where they're from!
   Your friend and
fellow thesper,
        Sylvia Miles.

Sylvia Miles

I BELIEVE IN ME

When I'm walking through this town
On the streets where I have grown
As they sneer and grin and smirk
'Cause they think I look berserk
While they laugh at what I say,
Scorn my life in every way
I can bear the shame, I know I'm not to blame
'Cause I believe in me, yes, I believe in me.

As they try to build on minor themes,
As I learn about their petty schemes,
While they so disdain my only dreams
I know it's not cool, they call me a fool
But I can bear the pain, I know I will remain
'Cause I believe in me, yes, I believe in me.

As they've tried to still and pacify
What is in my heart in mass supply
I have stood my ground, my head held high
I say without conceit, I'll not accept defeat
And I'll take all the strife, for it's my very life
'Cause I believe in me, yes, I believe in me.

from *ILL AT THESE NUMBERS*

Flap of images sworn
browning another purr
now warships slip sail
gone to trawl all grim
number and dead prices
poisoning the reserve
upon door long blame
and the old score cloak
flighty proof to dismal
then catastrophe loops
bending on the arabic
over crescents of zero

———

Prank shame rising
burns ice berg uplit
from flowing locks
turning loop scree
figure and end torn
the smile sun melts
who arrives for the
triple win bonus tip
upon dank defection
and so fills the arch
of the sent is a dune
brigade turning files

———

Tis neon now fiery crush
on starkest smithereens
squealing come rest track
as beaming traces show
lost pay to moth masque
and smugger captions
beguile each shut lively
now sent beyond in furs
or go garland the wrath
dice in hot dashing rivet
with hammy drills racing
on old warp factor blush
hand to geld wax mouth
spangled to windscreen
diamonds gone to crown
its veil in mergent blue

———

No more to sing Achilles
not a wrath bowl in strife
and frost dogs on shame
for all that falling spoils
tablets to lime composed
war on word fur on worse
the names we cannot sing
but no the scroll lays the
fatal stretch in huffy lays
stiff in etched epaulettes
shaking in a bloody sash
that softly crows of pain

IN THE WIND

Existing more with the cold frost
Strong as a cobweb in the wind
Hanging downward the most
Somehow remaining
Those beaded rays have the colors
I've seen in paintings—ah life
They have cheated you
Thinner than a cobweb's thread
Sheerer than any—
But it did attach itself
And held fast in strong winds
And singed by the leaping hot fires
Life—of which at singular times
I am both of your directions—
Somehow I remain hanging downward the most
As both of your directions pull me

Marilyn Monroe

O, TIME

O, Time
Be Kind
Help this weary being
To forget what is sad to remember
Loose my loneliness,
Ease my mind,
While you eat my flesh.

ROSIE'S POEM

you're
right
it's
a beautiful
wagon

low
weekly
rates

pile
a stones

the mystical
person
who is
my lover
in
Rapid
City,

today

hello
puppy
your magical
hair
at the
corner
of night
& lightning,

Motel 6
I always
think
of
the price
as the
temperature.

the 2 of
us
my shadow
my shadow

& lightning
over all
the
motels.

I'm curbing
myself

because what
isn't curb.

CLAIMS

i make a claim to the land it is mine, i make a claim to the land
              i hereby make application
                              for such share as may
be due to me of the fund appropriated by the Act of Congress approved June 30,
1906, in accordance with the decrees of the Court of Claims of May 18,1905, and
May 28, 1906, in favor of the Eastern Cherokees. the evidence of identity is herewith
subjoined.
              i, i choose owl. at this time. (this darkness that enters me is good, this
darkness that enters me closely) i make a claim to all the land and skies.
       i, Rhoda A. Martin, widow, Indian name unknown, through my great
grandfather Jerry Ward and his brother George Ward on my mother's side, claim
Cherokee descent. supplemental application for Eulalia she has lived with me since
she was 1 month old. her mother died in 1891 and gave me the child.

              i make a claim to the land as a spirit
              i make a claim to all the land, to share it with all other spirits and
              animals.
              i have nine other children of my own, dead or grown.
              i have countless children,
              i make a claim to the land as no one assert that it doesn't belong
              to any one. therefore i claim it
                              i have no name, i make a claim to the
land,
       it has no name, no part of the land has a name, to itself, your ownership of it
by placename and by tract is hereby invalid, the division into   stadiums
buildings rooms and other compartments.

              i make a claim to all the land i can fly over
              i make a claim for my children
              i make a claim for all spirits
              i make a claim for all animals.

killed us because they hated
us. sometimes because it amused them. thrilled them. yesterday they killed 100
civilians because they made a mistake. they are destroying as many stadiums
buildings rooms and other compartments as are left over from   the past years of
war. they appear to be unfeeling.

                              As birds which are ledge or cavity nesters the
owl's powers of building or repairing are either strictly limited or non-existent,

out of the darkness and striking the trespasser very hard. you have come too close
you have come too close   to me   and my nest
with your every action you have come too close   look at my face look at my
eyes   answer might possibly be, that their eyes are used to terrify their victims.
        Oh -o -o -o -o -o that you had never been bor -r -r -r -r -n.
have you ever been enrolled for annuities, land, or other benefits? if so state when
and where. yes in 1891. Lumpkin County, Georgia.
        the wild.

                    i know what that is, it's inside me
                    i don't have to claim it.
persisting with the treatment. Has the president been affected yet?
No? it may take time,
but damage is being done to him
look at my face look at my eyes,
        Oh -o -o -o -o -o that you had never been bor -r -r -r -r -n

A DREAM OF BACKED-UP DRAINS

1.

We came to the cathedral city of Köln on the wide Rhine River.
Never before had we come to the cathedral city of Köln on the
    wide Rhine River.
In drumming rain the great baroque cathedral rose over the
    rebuilt city of Köln on the wide Rhine River.
"Look!"—but no matter how high you cast your eyes
    you could not see the tops of the twin spires
    of the great baroque cathedral at Köln.

In the drumming rain, a smell of drains in the cathedral city
    of Köln.
The ruins of the medieval city rebuilt on the wide Rhine River.
The great baroque cathedral alone had been spared from bombing.
So God intervenes sometimes in the affairs of man.
So God in His caprice selects who will live, who will die.
Across the vast cathedral square of drumming rain and milling
    tourists there was a wish to believe in the God
    of the cathedral of Köln.

In our hotel room, top floor of the newly constructed Königshof,
    a view of the great baroque cathedral of Köln and a smell of
    backed-up drains.
In the bathroom amid the bright glittering tile, a smell
    of backed-up drains.
"Look!"—for in the tile floor near the sink, a drain
    measuring approximately nine inches in circumference.
An open metal drain through which you could see dark water.
Agitated water. In which something swam.
Unless it was vibrations.
A powerful smell rose from the drain.
A smell of time, a smell of raw life prevailing through time.
God is this power of raw, prevailing life.

A six-foot blond woman from the hotel desk came bringing BUZ FRESH
    aerosol and disinfectant and a small wisk brush.
A sound of faucets, and a toilet flushing.

Perhaps something was retrieved from the drain, or
    perhaps it was flushed away into oblivion.
"I am very sorry, these things happen."
The air was sprayed, a pungent floral scent. Out of the dark
    German forest, a sudden aroma of white lilies!

Carefully we placed the Köln telephone directory over the drain.
A smell of stopped-up drains prevailed in the cathedral city of
    Köln on the wide Rhine River, but we could no longer smell it.

2.

I had journeyed to Köln to give a public appearance.
It was my duty in Köln to present myself in words.
Yet we were in a desolate rural area.
We had been brought here, to be taken elsewhere.
Along a road, a truck with a dented fender moved toward us.
The driver stopped. He spoke only German, a burly man with
    strong hands and a close-shaved head.
His face was broad, frank and honest, modelled like a clay head.
His eyes shone flatly like polished glass.
Here was no man of mere language but a man of the earth.
Here was no man of mere poetry but a man of the people.
He would bring me to the place of my public appearance
    except I was not prepared.
I had misplaced my material, I had no words in any language!
That flimsy life raft upon which I'd imagined I might survive.
How quickly and shamefully I spoke. Yet there was an air of
    defiance in my voice.
I heard myself declare: *I am part Jewish.*
My family was Hungarian on my mother's side, and German Jewish
    on my father's side.
My German-Jewish great grandparents had emigrated to upstate
    New York in the 1890's. They'd settled in northern Niagara
    County. They'd changed their name from *Morgenstern* to
    Morningstar wishing to hide.

These remote facts I explained to the driver.
I had nothing to provide except my history.
I thought—*But I am not my history, am I?*
I thought—*But I am free of time, aren't I?*
Seeing the driver's strong hands I became agitated.

He was working-class, his nails were blunt and edged with dirt.
He knew nothing of poetry, of subtlety and subterfuge.
He knew nothing of my public identity, his instinct was unerring.
We were in such a desolate place!
What facts are there in history except *which place? which time?*
I was saying words I had never said before in any language.
"Please hold me, please be kind to me."
My ancestors spoke, through the gritty soil stuffed into their
    mouths.
His strong fingers stroking and caressing my head.
There was here the simulation of protectiveness as when a
    father, his thoughts distracted, nonetheless takes time
    to comfort a frightened child.
The driver stroked my shoulders, my arms.
I was only a child, I began to cry.
I was very frightened as only children in their wisdom
    can be frightened.
This is my dream! yet I could not prevent what would come next.
I thought—*I must behave with dignity.*
How surprised I would have been in my former life to see
    myself on my knees in this desolate wooded place!
The landscape was foreign like the language.
The soil was rough, though sandy.
The sky was the color of wet, wadded newsprint.
The wind smelled faintly of stopped-up drains.
At a horizon, a faint sun glowed like a hot coin.
The sun was a word for *elsewhere*, and *another time.*
When you looked to the sun hoping for more light the sun faded,
    like the fall into sleep.

On my knees I hid my face. I wasn't crying, I think.
The driver closed his strong fingers around my neck and
    began to squeeze, grunting with effort.
"Death by strangulation."

To be strangled is a terrible way to die, but
    I was not there for it.

Köln, Germany
6 September 1998

Ulick O'Connor

HOMAGE TO SEAN MacBRIDE (Died 16th July 1988)
(Winner of Nobel Prize for Peace and Lenin Peace Prize)

Always I remember you in that house
Standing at the door to welcome us,
The touch of the seigneur in your stance,
But the warmth of the chieftain in your glance.
Then, noticing as the night wore on
      How her presence filled the room[1]
      Like the scent of a faint perfume
That lingers after the beloved has gone.

In your talk legends were begotten—
"W.B. taught me English; Ezra, Latin".
And the mind recalled what the poet had said—
"That straight back and arrogant head".
In this forge she shaped what she held dear
      To free Ireland and release her sex
      From man-made laws, this was her text.
Constance,[2] Hannah,[3] Charlotte[4] all worked here.

You had the comprehension without which
There is no making sense of this crazy pitch,
How someone bred from high intent and creed
May tip the scales, unleash a fearful deed.
Yet had not that cast of mind prevailed,
      Slouched like a dolt beside the fire
      Savouring his anger like desire,
Would have let the pot simmer till it boiled.

In that book-lined room I watched many a night
You finger out a clause, begin the fight
To save some man; with dawn the firelight danced
On those high cheekbones, and the mind had chanced
On that fantastic knight; could one man find
      So much to joust against and win?
      Armoured with argument you went in,
Your lance the lightning flourish of the mind.

Now at your funeral a Cardinal talks,
Yeats' verses clamour through the vaults,
Lenin too, is named. So much has changed
Through you. At your grave the Army ranged
To present arms.[5] The same, which from your cell
      Took Rory to the firing squad.
      But that, too, has been turned to good,
More accomplished by a guiding will.

Through the streets the funeral takes its way,
An old woman grasps me by the hand to say—
"You could listen to her all night". That face
Again intrudes upon our space,
You and she in that great tale revealed,
      Which he thought alone worthy of theme,
      The people's book which holds the dream
When all that's left of Tara is a field.

[1] *Sean MacBride was the son of the beautiful and aristocratic Maud Gonne, whom Yeats wrote many well-known love poems to. She was a fighter for women's rights and Irish Nationalism and was adored by the Irish working classes.* [2] *Constance Markievicz (née Gore Booth), revolutionary. Condemned to death but reprieved for her part in the Rebellion of 1916. The subject of one of Yeats's finest poems. Elected to Westminster in 1918, Constance Markievicz was the first woman M.P.* [3] *Hannah Sheehy Skeffington, along with Maud Gonne and Constance Markievicz, was prominent in the struggle for Women's Rights and a supporter of the Suffragette Movement.* [4] *Charlotte Despard, one of the founding members of the Suffragette Movement in England and a sister of Lord French, Commander-in-Chief of the British Forces in Ireland. Charlotte Despard devoted the later years of her life to working for Ireland and lived with Maud Gonne in Roebuck House.* [5] *In the Civil War in 1922, Sean MacBride was on the Anti-Treaty side which opposed the new Irish Free State Army. He was arrested and shared a cell with one of the leaders of the Anti-Treaty forces, Rory O'Connor, who on 8th December, 1922 was taken from the cell and executed by an army firing squad as a reprisal.*

Joe Okonkwo

ENTITLEMENT

1925
He looked out the window
of his 125th Street apartment
and saw a hurricane raging:
it was raining cats and Jazz.

Langston was the gentle eye of the hurricane/
Zora, the force behind the hurricane/
and Duke, the royal who presided
over the hurricane and loved it madly.

He sauntered down 125th Street
in his tight double breasted suit
and two-toned shoes
like he was entitled to it all:
the Jazz streaming from the speakeasies,
the poetry smoking the air,
the black world on fire.

1967
His dashiki blazed like
African landscape.
His hair was big,
ferocious and safely
out of control.

King's staggering sermons
purred in his ears,
Baldwin's fire
ignited his brain,
his feet ached proudly
as he marched with
head, shoulders and
sign held high.

As he shouted anthems of protest,
Aretha's anthems of entitlement
wailed through him with gospel ecstasy.
A rock was thrown.
A battle ensued.
Water hoses materialized because
the black world was on fire.

2002
A doo rag adorns his head,
a smug crown.
His loose, baggy pants
hang half a foot
below his waist,
egregiously revealing underwear.

He swaggers through the streets,
parading his bad ass,
the songs in his head an ode
to drugs, prison, violence.
Bitter rhapsodies.
He is nigger to the core
and electrically proud of it.

He says what he wants,
does what he wants,
and fuck you if you
tell him he can't.
He is our future.
He sets the black world on fire.

Peter Orlovsky

AMERICA, GIVE A SHIT!
NEW YORK CITY—GET YOUR SHIT TOGETHER

You have to sit & think this thing out Peter—
How maney pounds does my city shit & piss a day?
How do we scoop it all up—collected?
& composted & brought back to farms
                              whear it belongs all along.
It's a great job & my pay is human manure,
                    I want a hundread pounds an hour
                    because I'm a hard worker,
                    or should I ask for more?
Always wanted to dig with a shuvel
                    in frunt our East Side Manhattan apt.
I know worm droppings are 15 dollars a pound.
I'll have to go study cities sewage blue prints
& dream of vacuum-flush toilets.
Remembering Allen & me walking to East River
                              around 17th Street
& there we saw the sewage flow about 2 feet deep
out 6 foot diameter tunnel
slowely moveing melting into East River.
What interesting surprise brown flow discovery,
          on its way to East Rivers garden floor.
Even cows dont throw away their plop
                    but let it drop
                    near many eating pasture spots
                    & next year dung turns into better green
                              grass than before.
Organic Gardening Magazine gets excited about reporting
China's engenuity in recycling 99% of the human manure
          of Shanghai's 14 million population
while Chinese farm girls in the field sing
                              odes to human dung
while raking more dried human manure
into the ground under persimmon fruit trees
as their babies sit nearby on the ground looking up
at the clear blue sky
listening to mama's human fertilizer song.

Jena Osman

from *MEMORY ERROR THEATER*

FACTS AND/OR FICTIONS $(\dfrac{1}{m})$

Memories are structures we create in order to answer to particular needs. What the memory in error reveals is the act of our subconscious choices. Once the act is exposed, it is possible for another choice to be imagined. Freud. Of course this wreaks havoc with identity. Think of the replicants in the movie *Blade Runner* who hold onto their photos as evidence of past lives they never had. When the photos are revealed to be fake, they are practically destroyed.

blade=*of grass, not leaves of. coming in contact on the ice pond and jaunty. the tongue flexes against the steel. the sword pushes us on, a cold front coming in and skimming. first the king's head, then the queen's. then the roundheads. then the peakheads.*

blade
              —not grass—
                                      coming in

ice pond

tongue
              —steel—
              —cold front—
                                      coming in

the king's head—

the queen's head—

$\dfrac{1}{m}$: the scene is a guillotine

DAY LOG ($\overset{\wedge}{2}$)

Sputter splint. Not getting around to it all day long. The "materials of revolution": what rule are you referring to? The story of the man who calls up another man and pretends to be a different one. This happens for two minutes before the different one is recognized as the man. Are physical markings materials? Are materials the actions of people? Weak synthesis is numbered paragraphs. A story of a man with a target scratched into his chest. The story of a man who left a final note while his company was under investigation. The walkway is a silver slide, almost a tunnel. Cutting the paper so it fits in the envelope. I just have strangeness. The story of the man (?) locked from pair-o-dice. The focus on their faces and youth. The man in the green suit is stabbed with a knife. Others are hurt with pool sticks. One location is another's dislocation. A man blows himself up on a bus. A man calls his dog Bonnie.

calls his dog=*Dogberry*: "Pray thee fellow, peace: I do not like thy look, I promise thee." *It's a grand mess-up.* "The defense team had said that the government had opposed the release of the information to spare it embarrassment over its mistakes, rather than to protect national security."

in$_2$formation

$\wedge$ $\wedge$ $\wedge$ $\wedge$
$\wedge$ $\wedge$ $\wedge$ $\wedge$

$\wedge$ $\wedge$ $\wedge$ $\wedge$

in$_2$forms
in$_2$former life
(*which life?*)

RELATIVISM (∧)

Under construction. Memory construction. Acknowledgement of the memory in error is not equal to denial of the real. *I did have some facts.* Because my three childhood memories were proven later to be false doesn't automatically invalidate all images that I retain from my childhood. The phenomenon simply illustrates that images continue to shift and change position in relation to experience as it happens. What we take in is instantly part of a dynamic cellular flow and reproduction. The columns are shifting; it must be an earthquake. No, it's a tremor. A continuous shudder. A city shrugs itself out of the shuddering shoulders of another. Remembering is not a duplicative process. We know it's fractured, but we grant it narrative status so we can feel our place is set.

cellular =

> *the comments*
> *in the pollen sac*
> *of an anther*
> *don't speak to each other or think*
> *of the semi-permeable mem-brain*
> *the winged nucleus of an insect divided by veins*
> *the electrolyte monastery*

(part)/

asking/
blink/
the dissected flame/

DAY LOG (☉)

The droning sound that wakes you then the room reverberates and the windows shut in order to keep out the breath that could kill you then a voice on the telephone details a dream then you open envelopes and steal those words then walk on a small stone then the tale of a dollar bill being passed from hand to hand then the "language of revolution" as a stale numerical list then pen and paper to show a commitment to remember then I remember the brick was actually a false front for a piece of wood then the message says "I'm not bitter" (that's a lie) then lights as technology and Faust in the supermarket then the sentences in circles as much less pleasant than the little dog knowing then everyone in the aisles with their ear to a call, forgetting.

What are the people like in that town? Exactly like the people in your town. A cage of awakenings. Toiling mesmer- and the pit-sea-stop.

lights as technology=*first angstrom and corpuscular bullying of the retina, then a secret illuminating agent. in spite of a small mental window, the discovery set us burning. amusing and spongy and slightly delirious. no cargo in debt to the spinnaker speed. guns and howitzers.*

set. us. burning.

WRITING TIME WITH QUOTES

December 31, 2002 remains on the alert trying to read Shakespeare's brain but it's slow going, with each attempt taking us farther away from any self-serve bones.

Cognitive science has lots to say to playground bullets circumcising the split subject, and can rescue a diffuse but real enough sense of accidental agency, which, even if 2% accurate, is enough to fatally contaminate a person's empirical bathwater. The sloshes provide some sense of motion between the ears, never forgetting the communicating vessels between legs, thus one stoops to be conquered by unconscious syntactic tactical groups, literate messengers repeatedly tearing back to report a sense of language as "profoundly alienating."

The way children of pidgin speakers form creoles is the way I write reading, at least it says that here, marking one pixel on the screen per conscious exhalation. But Gombich is right: that face in the mirror is half size.

Remember when it all meant? It hardly seemed fair that we, originary, omnipresent, unextravagated, were in history soup, kept out of the bubble by lovely archaic prayers from severed heads. There was money (but no benefits) if you could learn the programming to keep them current. Otherwise, go home, or homeless, both cases breaking open at the slightest smashes to reveal nation, pay its entertainment fees or go hungry.

George says "up is better than down" but who, tongue in one to two bodies and bodies in intellectual thrall to prior sky tongue (you say ideology, I say grammar) can tell which section of the sky will fall next. Meanwhile the eternal historical poetic command: Don't forget to register.

I now remember Creeley grinning as he quoted:

> And I could not help thinking
> of the wonders of the brain that
> hears that music and of our
> skill sometimes to record it.

119

Felice Picano

HIS SECRET
after learning of R.F.'s diagnosis

Questions are etched on the winter-garden's glass:
How shall one respond to what's already
been long known? How far, really, shall one go?

Everyone has fair reason to reveal—or to hold.
Still anxiety lies thick amid the flatware of Tea's
civility, outlasting games of Patience on the porch.

But what to say when the phone rings...just so?
Accommodation has so many drawbacks.
Couldn't one simply...get it over with?

...And so the mantle of once more being selected
for an unwanted secret clutches
the flinched shoulders of the "unaffected."

Once more, favors must be repaid, in triplicate
as, inversely, time passed in his company
trebles in value...and in complications.

For exactly how long, and in which situations
—being poured out or played out (quietly trumped)—
are you and I, already, little but memory.

WINDOW ELEGIES: L'ENVOI

It is not precisely as a whisper falls
seducing the dim air, there, where the inlet
pretends to be morning; no, nor the soft calls
of coins as they glitter in a goblet
you let smash. ...It lives between the bright
and the black, teasing your grasp, misted
like the mirror a dying man's spite
makes sigh, an imprint that barely existed.
...It is not an obvious loss, as though each day's lining
were unwound, each hair strung on a thread
blemish unfound, cache discovered in dread.
No. It is an address vanished, a name past divining
a costlier pain than you ever thought to possess:
Eons could not explain its sharp hold: its caress.

Pedro Pietri

INTRIGUING INSOMNIA
AT EL
HOTEL SPERINARI

Milaricano in Milano
mucho long way from
El Lower EastSide
where I do not reside

but live there
every now & then
among scattered ashes
of local legends

now feeding pigeons
in the square
of katholic Duomo
Sometime opens and
other times wonders

if the pigeons
are really after
bag of tourist peanuts
sold by the next
unrecent immigrant

to potential emperors
of foreign night clubs
opened all night long

while I reluctantly
write in misplaced
journal I keep losing

in amazing solitude
from hallway stairs
to the room for poetry
at the Hotel Sperinari

where the service
doesn't make the Poet
or the poem nervous
about not speaking
the same language

Porque because poetry
es universal slang
spoken by you and me
and whoever else is
unable to sleep tonight

not out of loneliness
or depression or
foreign acid indigestion

but because loss
of sleep can sometimes
be a rewarding experience
of late at night words
musical instruments speak

with the beat
of broken heart park
once upon lost times
of seat belt therapy
wall-to-wall paranoia

drinks were free
if you paid for them
proving you are serious
about being original,

maybe another poem
was not written
but poet felt at home
like the homeless do

when taking a nap
all over the world
anxiously and calmly
waiting for a phone
to ring in English

On Don Paolo's desk
At Hotel Sperinari
Lobby for foreigners
With tired suitcase
Feet looking forward

to resting in peace
if the price is right
and the night is long,

Don Paolo El Jefe
Immediately orders
His son Gianne Paolo
To spread the word
telephone call for

El one and unico
El Reverendo Pedro
El Poeta from
El upper Loisaida

Spanglish Attaché
Puerto Rican Embassy
For Domino comrades

Spanish Harlem
Anti urban hero
Dressed in black
for all occasions

Silently looking
out of memory window
for clues of last time
this trip was taken
from Midtown Manhattan

To Via Sperinari
neither downtown
nor uptown Milan
porque according
to my amigo Mario

is all about
el center of town
if you come around
for just a few days
to spend the night

At nowhere else but
El Hotel Sperinari
Not a major Hotel
But a memorable hotel

You will not find
on picture post cards
one mails back home
after leaving Italy

And you will return
if you are a Poet
followed by free verse
across the Atlantic,

Is not very romantic
to be alone in a room
if you are not writing
a poem and not letters

Stating how much
you miss being missed
when you are not missing!

but if poetry is
the reason you enjoy
so much losing sleep
in that hotel room
A long way from
Nuyorican Poets Cafe,

you will not complain
about loneliness
because to be alone
is not to be alone

therefore the mind
will not go blank
after the letter zzzzz
somewhere in Brooklyn

where museum meets
cemetery & love begins
to give you headaches
that are incurable
because you were warned
against making no money

Which meant
being a Poet who
is always falling
back on his rent

But did you listen
of course you didn't
listen to anything except
the bell that rings
on el manual typewriter

Otherwise you Poet
wouldn't be comfortable
losing unnecessary sleep
At El Hotel Sperinari!

Bongiorno Don Pedro
Bongiorno Don Paolo
Cappuccino por favor
Con grappa Correcto
To wake up the day

Nobody has to know
que you are un Poeta
in Milan to celebrate
publication of El
otro libro of poetry

translated from
Spanglish to Italian
by Amico Mario
who I met years ago
writing a book about
El Lower Eastside

where nobody in
their bilingual mind
can keep a secret
which isn't the case
this time and place

Unless there are
hotel historians
who cannot sleep
and want to document
to not hallucinate

& think they see
man dressed in black
from head to toes
wearing black hat
with an extra hand

attached to a black
walking talking cane
but don't think you
are going coming insane

it is just a poet
you are not seeing
refusing to take
the night for granted

it is more exciting
to lose sleep
all thru the night
of impaired vision
rewarding experience

where solitude can't
get more authentico
for a Nuyoricano
hotel Sperinari Poet
in El center of Milano

Milan, Italy, 2000

BLURB CUT-UP

moves through time/space with specificity and force

deep and quirky knowledge of the human soul

simultaneous exploration of the outside and the inside

the macrocosm and microcosm of the alchemists

Reclaims and re(dis)orders the Domains of Art

awakens long slumbering modes of thought

Vive la Révolution!

roots in our classical past

heart-blood of primordial humanity

remembers a time when we were watched by trees

the eternal elements of the poem: wind, sea, fire, death and love

brings these ancient powers close

sparkling, yet precise

a sweet ripeness

a vast dark promise

We come back to it

These poems use language like a can opener to breach the orders of thought with humor and urgency

questions that can only be asked within the poem

send us spinning

illuminating presentation

the radiance and emptiness of our own minds

a relevant—even urgent—text

Full of rich lore

will appeal to scholars and poets

some rapprochement

our "ancient future,"

a strong, bright lyric gift

full of music

the sounds of the streets

celebrates American lives as they are lived

relentlessly shows us the beauty in the world

presents us with coemergence

the dark and the light in our minds

a fierce, and honest portrayal of the struggle

realization

a journey home to ourselves

ceaseless as the cries of pain

blessedly unique

sacred tenacity

uprooted as we are on a vast and windy continent

the true and unwritten history of ideas

> New worlds of vision and language
> fleshed out
> the elegance and precision of organic form.

sophisticated innocence

our sense of wonder

the forms and orders of poetry

abuts the marvellous

in the sky of the mind new constellations

pied-piper alchemist mage cartographer

outrageous terrain of our secret odysseys

hard-loving hard-living city of poets

goofy, sublime stories

the eternal labyrinth

lucid and subtle

for simple, direct contemplation

the power of his heart-held beliefs

subtle, nonverbal experiences of realization

TRANSLATION 3

leaching modern life washes over human needs risen pointless charted off a child
in response to iniquities and failures being natural twins of fear removed from
delicate work done nature dances wouldn't see parts in these hills hawks compete
slanting intelligence ripped by the opening blast a frying pan wisps of dust in
rocking gullies shootouts trigger emotional upsets blood thickens, becomes sticky

leaching pointless put up of it natures humanly of it excess of them makes modern
required washing life card outside child in response to it that iniquities, and to them
will nutrition, which are naturally connected by it fear taken away delicate work
from them made dances of nature, it not to see that proportions of this falcons of
them, that were built, in order to belong intelligence in, that tore up by the
explosion of the opening wisps a tray bend of it from the dust in shootouts, by one
balanced of gullies roast around the light excitable blood of the revolutions to cause
thickens them, if becomes sticky

Bob Rosenthal

DEPRESSION: IT'S YOUR RIGHT!

Oomph! I fell off my sticky mat
1/4 inch high
I floundered on the floor eighteen months
I wouldn't stretch, I *wouldn't* no I *couldn't*
   get to the gym
but I could eat
   eat beyond appetite
eat till my belly obscured my shoes
eat till getting out a chair was aerobic activity

I like being depressed
nothing to do   with less feeling for others
no one to care about
everyone else is depressed
   angry   growly
now I have my own depression going
don't need love
don't need sex
can love my self enough
   big enough for two
enjoy freedom from vanity

if I get so happy that I forget I am depressed
I can look in the mirror
trapped on the floor on my back
    a turtle waving stubby limbs
can't get right side up

those who leapt from World
    Trade Center before it tumbled
found a 10-second extension fully felt
a positive step   out all the way

I stepped out of my perfect window

hoping to land in a support group
            instead taking my pants to be let out
funny movies are funnier when you're sad
money means less when life is worth less
I forgot I had anything but I knew I lost it
hoping someone would notice

it's a relief not to constantly invent
            means to happiness

fooling myself?
        or fooling around with myself?
I wasn't really depressed
couldn't get that straight
maybe I was just sulking
sulking good and long
sulks just don't last
infernal happiness does the dog in my brain
breathing is too much fun
even in shallow gulps

all you lucky ones   deep in your meds
unable to change
how I admire your steadfastness!
sulking is just the happy idiot's respite
depression however is your right

we are in the pit of the new millennium
sky is blue   breeze is warm
the war is on TV   the ground is approaching

I regret that this is the last of my lives
I am happy to toss you a line of two
making myself useful again
twenty pounds around my middle
to remind me of those good times
I too thought I was depressed

Michael Rothenberg

TAKE OUT

1.

words, all about words, poets,
all about poets and words and art, art
and poets and culture and civilizations

oh my god!

deep sigh chipping
away at corner of universe nobody believes in
as real as city lights strung chunks of gold
on full moon,

who'd imagine?
only me

2.

there's a great choir,
chorus of singers,
dead and alive, jazz band or orchestra,
rock and roll gospel choir, singing the blues,

under every nook and cranny
and no one believes they're there
because they don't frequently appear
as

marigolds
more as specters

optimistic true believers,
zen beatnik priests and priestesses
in no particular order

and though they fight amongst themselves
they make up in the end

3.

what is it I've come for?
        what primroses, roses, puffin, jack o'lanterns and fluff?

            WHEN DO I FINALLY GET FUCKED?

4.

You pray to god to win the lottery, win the Pushcart Prize for poetry,
        anything but this godforsaken world we know as
            POSSIBILITY that won't help you out
                of the rut you're
                in

                        sure, she says, go make a life, start over,

                        "You can do it Nicky!"

                    but fact of the matter is

            I'm absolutely, totally effectively, virtually, cyberly,
        modernly, poetically alone

5.

                    ready to burst, not

                because   life's too much

        to bare witness, not slowly

                    poison myself until I   hemorrhage,

                just ready to burst,

                        write a song from my own church

            THE CHURCH OF BELIEVE IT OR NOT

6.

Now you've heard about the generals

            cities and wars,
            snipers, terrorists,
            anthrax, ebola,

            AIDS

        How much are you willing to tolerate?
        Can you change it?

not from what I've been told,

        mala,
        Ganesh on Lucite lamp,
          Marble Balcony, TV set, stereo
         with demo light on, clock, electric outlet, glasses,
        secret insignia watch,
              tap it to make sure it's still TICKING

7.

      and I'm ticking,

wondering what my e-mail will say,
   IF someone will read my profile, find me attractive
   take me to Patagonia,

                  the bartendress, legal assistant,
          secretary, florist, masseuse, massage
       therapist, hypnotist, piano teacher, college professor

8.

I'm losing my poetry because I can't dream,

dreaming leads you down
a rosy path
littered with disappointment

9.

who can you trust?

what socks crumpled on floor?
what pillow case with pubic hair?
what towel to wipe counter and dishes?
two different towels or the same towel?

10.

bitch, hag, ogre, siren,

evil feminine spirit in the woods hides to seduce
crush your spirit so you become   slumped oversatisfied   lifeless drone?

GOODBYE CRUEL WORLD

11.

Gestures of kindness you notice,

speaking to the shriek of hell   soaring aquanaut,
playing field of Buddhas and Christs

Miami's pretty nice
It's hot, the people a bit displaced
I don't want to be here
when the last human breath is taken
in

12.

Beat up,

> I ought to order
> an eggplant parmigiana sandwich for dinner,
>> do something nice for myself, for a change

but I'm feeling a little bloated
because of all the string beans

> tap that watch again, make sure
> it's running

hell, why stress about it,
so what if it's your last

EGGPLANT PARMIGIANA SANDWICH?

October 25, 2002

138

WHERE JIMI IS

go now.
I used to follow you
you never could get rid of me.
now since you're dead
it's you
following me,
trying to escape that last exit—
the obsessive smelly
wet lips of death.
go now,
this is too long to wander.
1986 was your time.
go now.
it's not a devouring
void forever
black.
it's not gonna be like that, Michael
i promise.
death is where
jimi hendrix is,
where our revolution
ended up.
death—why mommy's there
and she has time
for you
now.

Sapphire

CREME WILD THING & KIWI GREEN

Yesterday I try to find some entry into what I love—
what I really like—it's black velvet, black period, Billie
    Holiday,
Ai, penetration, getting my cunt sucked, Dickens, "Killing
    Floor",
"Corrigadora", my work, the books I've had published, green
nail polish, the books not yet written, big niggers, kissing
blood, salt, meat, being held, taken in, flying.

This thing of pleasure, to identify the exact moment in flying,
when the plane accelerates and lifts the ground, what I love.
What I really want—to write like fucking war, kissing
the sun exploding, multiple births, cats & Billie Holiday
singing, "He wears high drape pants." Green
nail polish. Howlin' Wolf singing down on that killing floor

and "Who's Been Talking". When you know life is a killing floor
a hammer that comes down sending bits of bovine brains flying—
The colors are SHOCK, FLY GIRL, CREME WILD THING & KIWI GREEN.
Chocolate in one mouth, a man in the other, what I love
is as simple as what beats you, makes you fat, & Billie Holiday
singing, "My hair may not be curls," and kissing

You know it's so the opposite of cleaning houses, kissing.
For years I wondered exactly what a killing floor
was? The place the hammer met the forehead, where Billie Holiday
was raped when she was ten, the knife the throat, red flying—
a simple dinner, pasta garlic oil, lipstick, I love
doo wop sometimes, Sonny Till & The Orioles, the park green

the force of green, the plant tree osmotic green
eyes of this cat. Him holding your hand, kissing—
black lace, blood. Someone strong enough to hold the love
you give 'em, strong enough to dance on the killing floor
up to the hammer, giving life its due blood flying
like a flag. "When he starts in to love me," Billie Holiday—

"he is so strong and mellow!" To somehow sing like Billie Holiday
which would be to sing like yourself, all green
and soft and alive, the inside of thigh—open flying.
The lips tongue—thighs hands pressed kissing
the insistence introduction of life on a killing floor
born to die. In between if you're lucky love,

the force of green. Billie Holiday kissing notes, love
manifest in art. The penises' dance on that killing floor
between your dark mouth bits of your brain flying.

Sozan Schellin

SIX BLACK BOWLS
for Zenshin Philip Whalen, Teacher (October 20, 1923-June 26, 2002)

six black bowls[1] came down to me
through Baker,[2] Issan[3] and you
from Suzuki-roshi to my tan[4] in the zendo;[5]
today, it was orange juice in the bowl
from which your tomato juice flooded Tassajara;[6]
you warned us, Dharma[7] is like chewing on a tar baby;
you can't get rid of it;
and so with you;
the "old man" would always be there looking for licorice;
"atennyrate," in one swell foop
the koromo[8] empties itself;
smoke wafts in the zendo;
we kinhin[9] around seeking your poems,
"college cheese," "kow," now put away;
calligraphy from Hui-Neng[10] lining the drawer;
no dust under your bed; no mirror[11];
Kannon[12] embracing all from the dresser top;
Lou[13] ready to read again;
Ginsberg gone ahead, "irregardless," poems and sushi wait in your room;
silent sesshin,[14] except for thunder, here in Texas
where you came only to be with me

27-IV-2002

[1] *traditionally, the begging bowls of a Zen Buddhist monk* [2] *Richard Baker-roshi was Zenshin's Teacher* [3] *Issan Dorsey was Zenshin's Dharma Brother, and preceded him as the first Abbot of Hartford Street Zen Center, where I was ordained by Zenshin Philip Whalen, thus "relating me" to all three* [4] *a "tan" is a "place," a raised platform covered with a tatami matt, a zabuton and a zafu, two padded cushions used for support in meditation* [5] *the room or building where meditation is done* [6] *the monastery founded by Suzuki-roshi, south of San Francisco* [7] *the Buddha's Teaching* [8] *the outer robe of a Zen Buddhist monk, covered only by the Okesa [Buddha's Robe]* [9] *walking meditation, done very slowly in a circle* [10] *the Sixth Patriarch, author of the "Platform Sutra..."* [11] *see the "Platform Sutra of the Sixth Patriarch"* [12] *or Avalokiteshvara, the embodiment of compassion* [13] *Hartman, who read to Zenshin after he was completely blind* [14] *a silent meditation retreat, from four to ten days in length, with ritual eating in the zendo, using these bowls in the Japanese way*

from *THE NEW BABEL*

0

Babel of course is the fall of a Tower, followed by a vast, manipulated confusion of words.

Babble is language's beginning, before it's a language, while it's still song.

As Babel is both a ground and a zero, Middle English *grund* and Arabic *zefir*, *cipher*, Gallacized *zero*—let's call it Ground Zero.

Babel is defiance of the demiurge and hubris of the heart, ziggurat aimed at suns yet unborn, inside the mouth the mouth as desire: man creates gods.

Where before stood the North and South Phallus now yawns a smoldering Cleft, smoke subject to variable breezes.

The smoke contains bodies; we breathe one another. Thus, Babel is Kabul. We breathe one another.

As Ares broods over all the world's capitals: fragments of furniture spun from seized cockpits, strangers blinking into craters of Mars.

Babel is Kabul: Babel's a Bible in a motel room dresser in Birmingham, Alabama: Babel's the Battery Park Esplanade and the people still waiting in the airport in Santo Domingo.

Babel: the most beautiful girl in all of Kashgar, black haired, black eyed, maybe 13 years old, in a gay red dress, gazing admiringly at the foreign lady chance brought to her alley, gently, tentatively, mouthing a single phrase in English, addressed to that lady: "How do you do?"

Babel is mettlesome, its scrotum melted some, our mad extravagant metropolis, not bashful, still seeking the heights.

Babel was Mesopotamia, its era's only superpower: redound of Gilgamesh, modern day Iraq.

Babel is Baghdad, Babel is Belgrade, Babel's our backyard, a World that incessantly Trades names with itself.

Babble in three languages, babble in three thousand: put on a bib.

A baby babbled of lions eating books. And those lions ate books: Babel is books on the shelves of the Bibliothèque Queer.

No rabble in Babel: everyone's speech an equally valid muse. Thus: bomb them with butter.

Here is the blade with which Babel's abolished, here are the furrows where Babel begins, which no seed can boycott.

Babel rinses its parents in sorrow, Babel rewards its makers with slowworms, Babel is birth, rebuilding with cranes all sorts of crimes, the way life is a dagger, the way all wars begin with some bed's disaster.

Who shaved her cunt with Babel's boxcutter: born from the rubble, "ba" is for father, "ma" is for mother, sacred baboons patrolling her precincts.

Babel is Buddha dispensing with words, Babel is mating, thunder, whale blubber and rain, Babel is blame, Babel is ax, Babel is Bush-ben-Laden and fame.

As tall facades crumble like rockface, so many unbound mountains, Captain FBI simply offers "My bad."

Babble of waves, babble of wharves, of merchants and stores, city proud of its iron and brains: babble is braggart, babble is pulpit, babble's a word on the tip of your tongue or the trouble stored in a bull's flaring nostrils.

I'm down with the Tower of Babel.

I can't even enjoy a blade of grass unless I know there's a subway handy or record store or some other sign that people do not totally regret life.

Is stumble, is stutter, is stone smooth as skin, towers swaying the way they sway in the wind, as a person is always his tongue's own half-witting puppet.

Is the baker whose pancakes are unscaleable, whose loaves are uncanny and sprinkled with pain.

Is flesh covered with brine, is bitumen cracked with fever, wolves in the blood howling to the gibbous heart.

Babel is the beaten ballplayer who goes ballistic; Babel is an icicle in your mouth as melodious as a flute, as percussive in its dripping as drums.

Tower whose twisted tendrils resemble trellis and grapes, destruction demanded by the Dionysus of east meeting west, an unwillingness to consent to any loss of the self.

Babel is nothing but the celebration of words, talk armed with torches, dreams capsized by bigger dreams, the truth of each crater, the "bang bang" that wakes one from dream, the gap between "it's an accident" and "my god it's intentional," the B1 Bomber they're building and building, the backlash and the backlash to backlash and the backlash to backlash to backlash, O Barrio of Barriers, *our* republic of fear.

Enough elasticity to move with the wind, enough stiffness so that people can't know the building is moving: Babel is bubblegum stuck to your face.

Babel is presence, Babel is absence: nothing but the celebration of presence. *No mas* to sacred explosions, *no mas* to the occupation of land: sacred explosions, the occupation of land.

Babel is how a man howls as he leaps from the heights, where no other man can hear him; Babel is that moment of imagining one can fly, a brevity that lasts forever in Babel's unconscious.

Babel is a ray of sunlight crashing earthbound, a rivulet of rays crashing earthbound, a field mined with light.

The Tower of Babel: word up.

If architecture is frozen music, then these melted, smoking shards are its melodies, its incandescent burial grounds—Babel becomes what begs you to sing it.

Sudeep Sen

LINES OF DESIRE:
TEN MOVEMENTS ON EROTICA

1. INDIAN DESSERT

Clumps of smoke simmer in the pan, and slowly
   lift to caress the outline of your breasts

as you cook, stirring spices in carrot, milk,
   and cream—ingredients that conjure

recipes of hunger and passion. As you stroke
   sugar and butter and gently melt

flakes of grated almond-shavings,
   more clumps of perfumed smoke permeate through

the silk of your shirt—now transparent in heat—
   painting the outer circle of the nipples

to an hardened edge, tasting the sweet
   skin, the surface of the crinkled base,

to a creamed mouthful of untampered delicacy.

* * *

2. ABSENCES

Our mattress is the wide ocean,
   crushed sheets, the waves.
We sail together, full blown.

But during your long absences
   as our ships are docked
on different shores, sometimes

the bed dreams: I imagine, the wet
  breaking the anchor loose, defying
gravity, current, and electricity,

photons that propel and burn
  even the wild salted expanse
into a monument—a desire—

permanent like the ocean bed,
  its pulses uncontrollably rocking:
the waters, the bodies, the dreams.

     * * *

3. DESIRE

Under the soft translucent linen,
  the ridges around your nipples

harden at the thought of my tongue.
  You, arched like an inverted letter 'c'

move yourself deliberately
  wanting the warm press of my lips,

its wet to coat the skin
  that is bristling, burning,

breaking into sweats of desire—
  sweet juices of imagination.

But in fact, I haven't even touched
  you. At least, not as yet.

     * * *

4. TASTE

Our skin
   breathes love

through
   its pores,

glands
   transforming

shivers
   into taste.

Taste
   of desire

is the taste
   of its warm

lingering
   after-taste.

* * *

5. LYING BARE

Your bare stomach
   is my pillow.

When I turn
   my head

on one side,
   warm air rises

from the valley
  to lull me;

on the other
  side,

you shield my sight
  of your face

with your bosom
  to devour me

in the gorge
  near your heart.

        * * *

6. MORNING

  Buried in warm skin
toasted in the night's passion,

I struggle this morning, to emerge
  out of this heavy air.

        * * *

7. DAY BEFORE SUMMER SOLSTICE

We are sealed in marriage today
  to celebrate
tomorrow: the earth's longest day.

We are mere stardust of an ancient
  supernova, one that gave
us our metal, blood, and breath.

        * * *

8. CLIMAX

Lips
of a rose-
  bud
open
  to let
the dew
  drop
in.

* * *

9. RELEASE

The stamen
  raises
its head,
  bursting,
to shed pollen:
  relief-
rain
  showers
the parched
  folds
of pink skin.

* * *

10. KISS: AN HAIKU

a languorous kiss
  the faintest smell of ocean
salt-lipped breeze, pleading

SPIDERDUCK
from *VOG*
for Robert Kelly

red sun

over

Mud Island

(Sun Studio

a monument to

itself)

"Redemption"

shouts
the sign

over the station
for change

in
the casino

Rae-
ification

My eye
scans the chipped

plywood surface
of the old

portable stage
noting

the uneven
distance between
galvanized nails

As tho swimming
were a solution
so harsh

in the text
Vowel
hidden

in Trakl
Homo
erotics

of Peter
Pan
muted

woman assigned
to play
the boy

Wounded
Acres
But the father's

name is Jumbo
Introduction
of the ball point
killed penmanship

In the distance, in
some other room
a telephone
doesn't so much ring as

give a soft
electronic yodel
The secret
end of any

year is
Christmas,
the week after
mere echo

Cowboy
leans against wall
of two-story
res hotel

Colin
Owl,
king
of the night forest

The logout
beckons
as the login
beckoned,

memory
is a kind of
chip
Broccoli
is a mustard

(eat your tree)
Mime field
Days outstanding
Bert and Ernie:
don't ask,

don't tell
Geese demand
their favorite poet
Bronk Bronk
False tart,

scone head
Often I am permitted
to return to a method
as if to a mind: mine
A blind man talks

to the mailbox—
how am I to interpret this
Hannah calls to complain
that I failed to warn
she was about to fall

I blinks
Explain
that this cloth doll
represents the bear
but as an ideal

with no equivalent
in nature Refer
to this notebook
as a pen-based
system

Absence of tumor-markers
discernible in the blood
Putting the punk
into punctuation
(bad to verse)
an old man with infant sons

each drinking
from a plastic bottle
diluted apple juice
pushes the twin stroller past
the blue house whose
garage (dark, deep)

always sits open
one half dozen
American sedans

each in its various
state of repair
hoods up, wheels off, door

missing—and to the side
shining, brilliant
inexplicable in this
residential neighborhood
their own
Coca-Cola vending machine

Catfish sullen
at the bottom of the tank
The joy of disjunction
Yesterday's snow
waterfall frozen
at the man-made lake

Tragedy of the dream
in the peasant's bent
ballot   Puzzle pieces
strewn over the carpet
Family of deer
walk slow over the snow

An African gray
is a parrot
that one in the blue cage
reciting your own lines
back to you
in alternate accents

Hibition
Crows swarm at dawn
Between Eros and
erosion
memory enters in
A voice is calling
Daddy

Dog watches suspiciously
as I lean over the notebook
Desktopia
The bitter batter
of Little Feat
Life on the phone
Red dog on a blue tree

Macro to determine
break in the line
Each frame
of Zapruder's film
known by its number
Wasps bounce
off thick plate glass

nine stories up
second tallest building
in Waco
as I stare
out across town
all the way to the lake
When he says "we"

he excludes himself
Read at Discovery Zone
At Home Depot an entire wall
of linebreaks   I look up
in time to see her standing
staring out that eighth story
window (from my

perspective one frame
in a tall glass wall)
wearing not a stitch
scratching, one breast
missing entirely
Three squirrels gallop
across an open field

as they never will
in the city
High in the oak tops
a woodpecker heard
but not seen
Desire as a noun vs.
desire as a verb

When the King of Prussia
mall expanded
from six anchor tenants
to nine, auto
thefts in the lot
of the Lockheed Martin

plant across Mall Blvd
rose from two
per year to
six per month
Inside the train
the horn sounds distinct

Station
of the Métro
Apparition
of a pistol
against a wet black brow
I see her pausing

to look up
as if in thought
by the galvanized
can at
the driveway's end
My text

instead of an onion
Old man wearing ear muffs
and thick gloves walking

round the high school track
The year horizontal stripes
showed up in

everybody's logo
(3D effect)   I slept
watching the plan
ning commission on
the community access
cable channel

right thru
the amendments
to the environmental
impact report
Red brick light

industrial district
Tea spilled
on trousers
goes from hot
to cool

in an instant
Writing is a maid
to Emory
considering how exaggerated
the paranoia is

Translucent morning moon
Nature used
as a figure
of emotion
Conjunction understood

as punctuation
A Greek chorus
of mice for a tale
of a pig that
thought it was a dog

Bruised Andrews
Powder
over slosh atop
ice: geology
of January

Chasing chickens
Choosing
thickens choice
Red tail dips

pursued by crows
high above
Phoenixville Pike
Chinchillas

gone now
entirely from the wild
The cow before
it was domesticated

Force
of the plane
in the way
it brakes

Open the
sandwich
to strip out

onion
Fake Falls
Having thunk

With a thud
the house shudders
and the furnace

ignites
First light

the silhouette
of trees

already

visible

the large
dark blocks

of houses
beneath them

but the sky
barely discernible
Behind me

a man recounts
his having bought
his teenage

nephew
a shotgun, who
receiving it

said only
"I thought
it would be
automatic"

Ear
understood
as a culture
for infection

From pretest
to protest
Nail torn
beneath the quick

Egrets stomp
through reeds
in the swamp
Objects

in text appear
closer
than they are
Rain
on the surface

of the lake
Storm distorts
fountain's spout
Six flights below
boat tail grackle

screaming in the trees
My gars
and starters
Arms, legs
spread wide

asleep in a large bed
Yarn to web
each piece of furniture
is called "an invention"
My rabbit lies over the ocean

Fat wet flakes
of a spring snow
        Woodpecker
paradiddle
That which is

merely
positional
shall soon root
Teen mom
pauses in the mall
stroller

crowded with bags
Weekday morning supermarket
crowded with old men
At the service
station
a man in a brown

jumpsuit
slowly waves
a customer into
the proper bay
Atop a wood pole
mailbox

capped with snow
Elevator
as a trope
for civilization
Backside
of row houses

old brick from wch
hang slantwise
half collapsing
tar paper
porch rooves
Two women

talking loudly
rapidly
almost simultaneously
the first in
French
the other

English
When she showed him
the small silver
ring in her nipple

he slipped
his little finger in
& gave it a tug

Under the old bridge
dry creek bed
filled now with tires
Why the red-
bellied wood
pecker has
so much more

red at the back
of the head
Young couple
with an older man
for lunch
in a SoHo bistro
create

in themselves
a completed narrative
(fill in the gaps)
until, dessert plates empty
they pay and rise to leave
and I realize
now for the first time

the older man's with her
Chickadee at the suet cake
How quickly
this blue sky clouds over
Rain spilling over every eave
Squirrel dangling upside down
from bird feeder

spinning on a chain
Between cars at the stop light
he walks holding high
the crude cardboard sign

"I do not," it reads,
"steal or rob
so please help

the homeless"
Try to recognize
that familiar face
who with her tongue plays
at your foreskin
in the dream
Catfish swarm

at the water's surface
under the bridge
lured by a handful
of dry cat food
First tulips, first hyacinth
forsythia's yellow bursts

against the grey wall
of winter forest
Small boy dances
to inaudible tune
while a large
but immature

puppy nuzzles
into the dirt
Orange triangle –
danger –
on the back of
the otherwise

black buggy
filled
to absolute capacity
by the Amish man
and his children
Discern

by the shape
of the woodpecker's
head
      Coolest
in the basement
on a hot night

Yard thick
with the odor
of mulch
Scatter
of magnolia
petals

at the base
of the tree
the taller
poplars
still bare
and grey

Why rabbits
won't eat
dandelions
Noisily farting
That each line

on its own
must stand
or else
People
come up to me

and tell me
their dreams
Man standing
by a blue car
the hood up

in a light rain
A walk at dusk
amid flowers
to the distant
chortle

somewhere of a jay
A woman
sits cross-legged
next to a row
of newspaper racks

checkerboard smile
the pupil of one eye
clouded over
Try to catch
sun motes

in the palm of
your hand
Birdlike
warble
of distant car alarm

Quesadilla space monster
Hotel room john
sink used as a
desk to write on

Moon shadow shoots
through the kitchen
long tail just visible
going out the door

Four is to seven as
verbs to nouns
clutter the mind
A large book

to purchase in hard back
Pen perceived
as marketing tchochke
 by Lexis-Nexis

Rock band in bar
downstairs curiously
slow or quiet
Back when I

imagined Smithson
as "older"
Calamari writhes
between my teeth

We put the pro
in Prozac
The new sentence
as an adult

"Quote me, please,"
pleads David Bromige
"Oooh," groans David Melnick

I walk along
the thundering J car
tracks, shops lit

up bright for the night
old hash joint
now become

bright Boston Market
(née Chicken)
In a bookshop

poems by Sandy Berrigan
inscribed "Dear Philip…"
It's 5:15 am

in some other time zone
"Well, she can't dye
them eyelashes"

Large woman ambles
straw bags in either hand
heavy with groceries

(bread stick jutting
out like a flag)

while ahead
two boys race skipping

Another woman's
blonde dreadlocks

over deep dark
African checks

accented
by a neck brace

Latest euphemism
Skilled Nursing Facilities

called in the profession
SNFs

Sip gunpowder tea

in a room of shadows

the gamelan strictly

in your head

while outside

the Kampuchean girl

is turning cartwheels

GRINGOLANDIA

It's what Hungary was for the Viennese
or Romania for old Romans; those who
were once filthy rich can still afford
to be dissatisfied and surly; the retired
or failed can get creative with their past,
then resurrect as actors, painters, poets
—like Socrates or CEOs in prison;
those who've never in their lives been
hungry can undertake fantastic diets
or lecture on The Hungers of Our Times.

We are all born-agains through the wonders
of perjury, conversion or cosmetic surgery.
One ingénue may have had three face lifts,
each one following a will or a new alimony.
The play's director, (commander of the town's
American Legion Post) cancelled the opening,
flying to Holland for a shipment of cocaine.
Our friendly neighborhood murderer is giving up
his weekly column, "Jailhouse Cooking,"
to open an antique shop with his mother.

The rich come for two weeks every year
at least, visiting trophy mansions, their own
museums to a life someone almost like them
must have lived. As for living,
the servants do that for them. Housemaids
wash and hand-iron the unsullied bedsheets,
or on vast, bare tables arrange cut flowers
that the gardener's just gardened. Upstairs,
bedlights and radios flick themselves off or on
in warning: somebody could be home.

The natives prove useful—offering occasions
for good works and those inspiring causes
that fill up long, do-nothing days. Although
we do scold any neighbor who overpays them,
there is something we must still admire
in how we forgive them for inbred dishonesties:
("Why call the police? —*they* already know!")
We should invite some few to parties and expound
indigenous mythologies for them, recommend
strong home lives as the alternative to migration.

SNOW FLIES, BURN BRUSH, SHUT DOWN

A wide line of men in the open pine woods
diesel torches   dripping flame
lava soil   frost on the sagebrush
loggers walking from brushpile to brushpile
dark sky reddish from brushpiles burning.
At Sidwalter Butte three men on horseback
torches mounted on slender lances
crisscrossing miles of buttes and canyons

hundreds of brushpiles aflame
steady light snow.

end of the season, Warm Springs, Oregon, 1954/2002

Onna Solomon

FUCK LITERATURE

Bend me over a proverbial table
or a real table, whichever you prefer
and whisper to me:
            "It serves
        our words
                and bodies
            in rhythms
                of breath
            and skin,"
while we lie
like a white mountain on a white sea
my chest against the cold formica
of all tables, all fables of lust and language.
Poetry, make me come
to the place where all souls are naked,
where our words copulate
like voices in a two-piece harmony.
Fuck Literature.
This is not a metaphor, a simile.
This is not *like* that
or *as if it were* that.
This is this: pen and paper.
Consummate this relationship.
Dickens must have been a poor romancer,
taking too long to get to the good love,
working his way, word by expensive word,
to the verb of love or lick or
tie me up to the bedpost,
lubricate me with a sonnet.
You can compare me to a summer's day:
the hot heat beating on the bed,
the sweat of a good long hard journey
to where climax meets resolution.

The solution to frustration
of blank mind, blank page
is to engage in fellatio, cunnilingus.
Wrap that tongue around that word,
pull the blank look off the page,
make it stare into your eyes.
The surprise of connection:
erection of the noun by the verb.

Sparrow

SELF-HELP POEM

Are you pre-rich (in other words, have you not yet made your fortune)?
Pay attention to this poem, and you will soon be post-rich...
    or, to be exact, a millionaire!

There are seven secrets to becoming post-rich:

1) hard work
2) proper facial expression
3) "mental additives"
4) the right boyfriend, or girlfriend
5) good diet
6) correct music
7) study of the Scriptures

Let me explain further:

1) Becoming post-rich is not easy. Supreme effort is required.
2) If one studies the faces of millionaires, one notices certain similarities: strong, sure features, far-seeing eyes, a certain "squareness" in the center of the face. Begin to cultivate these features in yourself.
3) "Mental additives" means that your mind adds to what it sees. A pre-rich person sees a store, or a mountain; a post-rich person sees the flow of money.
4) Becoming post-rich is a journey; your boyfriend, or girlfriend must make it with you. Are they prepared?
5) Food feeds your energy-level. A poor diet creates a poor woman (or man).
6) Many pre-rich people sap their vitality with wasteful music. You require music that keeps you on the post-rich path.
7) You need not be religious, or spiritual, to be post-rich; however, you must read the Scriptures. Every millionaire has studied the Scriptures. These books contain valuable secrets of wealth.

There is much more to learn! This poem contains 186 more stanzas!

Call 1-800-999-1112 for more information.

William Strangmeyer

CHANGE OF SEASONS

Again the winter's soon to come and the daydream changes
to a line of trees and not garments slipping off
over smooth and hairless arms and legs with cornered
knees and elbows, feet like machines. Pornography
gives way to nostalgia and steel and the gang of craggy old faces
sitting in thin sun is a line of trees and the entry line of a forest,
an infinite line of trees and infinite depths, all the way to Norway,
and peopled by creatures of clay and by creatures of ash,
sand among the pines and here and there a child's lost wagon,
left behind when the child was lost, a cast off pupa
to be eaten by a bear while the adult imago goes off chewing,
molted and chewing on a loss and hunting huge, fierce things
that hate the pornography of summer because it doesn't fit
in their filthy official envelopes and obscene lines of death.
But that's a distraction! On to the Russian peninsulas!
We shall eat ice and snow! We shall await the time of mud,
the time of mud and hope as we drink,
drink wooden-flavored warmth and read our books on horseback,
battling the dark and the darklings who drool ashes from maws.

Todd Swift

PENTHOUSE REVISITED

What is it I really want from them: caught
licking a fine, full-globed, demi-tanned tit,
interested cupping an umber, saliva-tipped
nipple in a red-nailed clutch, curled fingers,

their lace skirts hiked up to spider-silk taut
inner thighs, sun-browned or goat's cream
pale, to reveal a trimmed, diamond-shaped
slit, pearled with audacity, their stockings

charcoal grey, or scarlet, pushed half-way up,
in smeared light Master Vermeer himself
would've wept to apply—with such intensity,
as the strokes imbue *Vaseline* with properties

that almost earn claims of artistic integrity?
Why do I wish to move in tonight, just so,
to their plentiful houses finely decorated
in French Provincial, or American Gothic,

as if a connoisseur-slattern subscribed
to *Better Homes and Gardens*, had stocked
a whole house full of boudoirs filled with
copious feather-spilling bolsters for lesbian

sleep-overs, and four-poster beds for Sun
King-sized brief encounters, and wrought
iron bedsteads for kerchiefs to playfully tie
slim, girlish wrists to—but not too tightly?

Why do I respond stiffly, as if to patriotic
hymns, when I alight upon such pictorials:
she's toting black sunglasses, nothing else,
her cocoa-buttered, navel-ringed torso laid

over a simply blazing turquoise backdrop
of parrot-green palm and chlorinated blue,
or in the hot horse-dusky barn, on hay bales,
she fingers her bumhole, beneath a frilly

violet bonnet, legs swinging loose in a yellow
summer dress, sweet under a Georgia willow,
fresh from a debutante's ball, or slave auction?
Is it only that, in seeing all of them still there,

in their never-changing, ever-available poses:
arched, semi-reclined, or dangling upside-down,
after so many decades away from when these
women were my yearned-for implausible lovers

(no more likely than Hitch's heroine, Novak)
stuck under my bed, pressed like meaningful
leaves or petals in a book, but here between
mattress and cold box springs—I am nostalgic,

brought back, like at Tintern Abbey, to earlier
awkward vertigos, on puberty's bridge of sighs—
and find myself, oddly renewed here at this web
site, after all my actual partners' genuine touch,

human insight—left to pause, praise and collect
these thumbnail scans of mere images of Eros—
adore their flat, impervious, imperishable teases
that were promises of the little that is so much?

Eileen Tabios

HELEN

Part of mortality's significance is that wars end.

Yesterday, I determined to stop watering down my perfumes.

Insomnia consistently leads me to a window overlooking silvery green foliage—
tanacetum argenteum—whose species include the tansy which Ganymede drank to
achieve immortality.

Once, I could have been tempted.

But to be human is to be forgiven.

The man in my bed shifts, flings an arm across the empty sheet—gladly, I witness
him avoid an encounter with desolation.

Soon, summer shall bring a snowfall of daisies across these leaves whose mottles
under a brightening moonlight begin to twinkle like a saddhu's eyes.

I can feel my hand reaching to stroke the white blooms as gently as I long to touch
a newborn's brow.

By then, I swear my hand shall lack trembling.

I am nearly done with homesickness for Year Zero.

This is my second-to-last pledge:
insomniac thoughts understate my capacity for milk.

This is my last pledge:
I will not drink until all—all of you—have quenched your thirst.

EYE SHADOWS

All aristocratic men wore makeup at the court of Louis Quinze.
The seducer Lovelace looked foppish but was lethal.
Since then, men's cosmetics have taken a precipitous fall.
Now he's ill-tempered as she struggles with her mascara.
In the moonlight, no one wears makeup, and if there's blush left on her face, it's
    blanched out.
She sits on him, and he's her rocking horse, familiar, steady, silver.

Judith Taylor

SMALL HOUSE

I stand at a window in a room with my love
watching the river

    try to move out from under a blanket of ice

The Japanese have a word—*aware*—the moment of joy
    infused with the sense of impermanence

Each moment containing its own epitaph

    A place where memory etches itself on

        delicate paper

Thomas R. Thorpe

FROZEN TEARS

*Save the page.
Turn the
corner.
Safety does not
last. Wish upon
a stone.
Is man trapped
by understanding
or punished
with self
knowledge?
Don't forget to
write. In dreams
the dead
speak little.*

33

How can I dry these frozen tears trapped in
adolescent fear of becoming what
I already am, a sober
man of 33? Not
unlike my father
who died at 46,
alone in his
coma, never to
say *goodbye,
I love you*
or *go for* it
again. In
January Satie's
chords fall to
Parisian streets,
and it snows, as
it sometimes does.
Thinking of the tracks
I left across America
leading far, far away, from hospital beds,
nursing homes, rehabs and cemeteries,
I've said my peace now,

not as then.
Expressed my concern and
prayed for the other
alcoholics nested
deep in refrain. 13 is
an age as 87 is
another. Somewhere
between the death
of one and the
life of another
lies the chorus,
chords falling

*Here upon earth seldom
does understanding meet
with expectation as
sadness garnishes
Happy Meals and
c i g a r e t t e s ,
hospital linens
and BMX.
Stand to say
goodbye.*

as the melody goes
whistling ...

Awake at last.

Thomas R. Thorpe

NEURALNET

Serenity becomes peace.

Patterns emerge as

dark matter shapes light.

Trees spider to deep nebulae;

filament of imagination,

manifests through birth.

Illusion of Illusions,

destiny of origins.

Fragile as an orchid,

your spirit in flesh.

Now, you must choose.

Live amongst stars

or fill the void with absence.

To survive here

one must become light:

the last sunrise on
The Argonauts.

Or return now
to mortal eternity.

A choice,

simple as

an infant's first breath.

CHAQUE FOIS

The circumstances of
my   disappearance   are
unclear
a loose wire sparking the
morse intervals of a lost
connection a sharp crack the
pulse or then and then with
each   the   singularity
consisting in the once just
once *chaque fois cette seule
fois*
More elaborate methods are
required   whose   mere
enunciation means to be
exposed
When the light falls Come up
—and to "science"—and
reciprocity I apologise In the
face of the monumental
comprehend   the   slow
curvature of each one in
particular The palm the back
They have been told: The
animal pole is anterior If
some bread be moistened and
kept
yet an other
thing grows An example
The   condemnation   to
freedom If I say so then the
fragment Such a will, as self-
presence, would instead lose
the *ground*

They collapse
To skin: for
their   bodily   shape   is
maintained   by   the   current
often and
silently   and   because   it   is   a
question   of   measure   I
contract in their presence
the distain the

    sight   of   the   world

And afterwards
It   is   never   spoken   *For
emerging   from   us   it   changes
us*   There   is   no   purchase   these
enigmatic   bodies   At   37.5°C
are   warm—pliable   wasted
still   we   are   forced   to   suspect
existence   having   exhausted
the   store   I   can   only   speculate
the taste respect the
dead   One set of tracks
will   lead   to   a   body   [is]   the
other will be redoubled

THE THEORIST HAS NO SAMBA!

there is a new instantism > a language of tangent =
tanguage > ambient funguage > there is a modern path
> invented through accidental spontaneity + of mock
language sport = fractured intelligentsillys > there
are sage athleticists + important children farmed out
to the furthest reaches of nowness > ... > ... >

I propose a New Instantism. Take spontaneousness out
of the ether and smack it into the throes of the wild
screaming bastard maggot that IS poetry! I propose a
New NEWness, where we refuse to comply by the aged
fumblings of mere MEANING and instead descend into
mere HEARING! I instigate a NEW failure of
listening...so we may one day walk hand in hand with
our own ears and say...THANK THE MIGHTY LOUD THAT I
MAY THANK THE MIGHTY LOUD THAT I MAY THANK THE MIGHTY
LOUD! I have a NEW Instantaety, a modern NEWness, a
post NOWism...I have a fear...of hiding this fear,
instead...I choose a revelry of failure, an opportune
dementia into the song of my pacifism.

Let's say we level expectation with implied tension.
The instant doubt appears, possibility appears next to it as a window.
What was thought to have clarity is now diffused by possibility.
Is possibility the goal...or only the instant before doubt?

The New Instantists will allow possibility room to
doubt itself...inventing a paranoia into the sleepless
monster that is this bastard maggot poetry. The New
Instantist will know that it takes a flat surface to
iron out procedure, that a wrinkled pair of favorite
pants will match an equally wrinkled ass...and mind.
That no matter how just or unjust the outcome...the
New Instantist will always be blamed for what has just
happened! Occurrence...being the signpost
for all things instant.

To what is now
And what is never then
To what has been
And what will never now
To things all thinging
And soon all soon'ing
To what is now
Instantly now

John Updike

TREES

Mute massive entities
that make no claims on me
beyond the odd acorn
pinging my car roof or
the drifts of autumn leaves
demanding disposal, trees
evolved life-properties
quite unlike mine—less nervous,
statelier. The bast
and cambium pass sap
from root to leaf and back,
and mute cells multiply.

Their leafy heads contain
wind-motions but no brain;
their heartwood holds them firm,
unweakened by a qualm
of love, forethought, or fear.
For many million years
insensate trees played host
to borers, birds, and rust.
They breathe out oxygen,
the gas that we take in,
and suck in CO_2,
which our lungs find *de trop*.
Benignly then, each tree
in sweetly breathing keeps
our fevered planet cool
and, manwise, liveable.

And yet, en masse, their aura
in darkling grove or forest
feels hostile; silent hate
is what they emanate,
tough trunk and branching claw
protesting ax and saw
and traffic noise and fumes
that shrivel verdant plumes.
Pickets within the strife
brute matter thrusts on life,
trees mother us by day,
but nightly mourn our sway.

Phillip Ward

JULY FOURTH
for Gregory Baines, 1964-1997

"No one commits suicide: everyone is killed."
—Julian Beck

down beneath the blades of bluegrass
a sweet green heaven has taken root
his body pumped full of formaldehyde
and swollen like a balloon his head rises
on certain earth-moving occasions
he wonders why he is here blind and
dumbfounded by perpetual darkness
in a quiet unlit satin-lined box

death came quickly for him
with a polished gun placed firmly
against his young curly-haired head
in one quick flash a hammered bullet
raced through the warmth of his head
where the barrel of a chrome-plated gun
was the only truth and final act of being
of my mortally-terrified little brother

Phillip Ward

POST-SESSION 23
for Amy Polley, 1956-1997

comically we hatch before the dawn of morn
quaint sighs gasp the new breath of life
and squinting eyes swallow prisms of the sun

lost in thoughts one becomes a trigger of dreams
of what he was lives away realms long forgotten
and squeezes memories into rainbows of eternity

lackadaisically we all become the searchers of
yet never quite knowing the *of* of ourselves
not until realities and scratched mirrors are cracked

when do we become ourselves in this lifetime
or is it in the next that we meet the challenger
and lose the context of dreams spherical discoveries

what with the mirror's double image of the self
the sojourn of being not really here or was
and is it real a fantasy these lives we have

red-rimmed eyes speak the sorrows of living
as we know it but within the soul of itself you
and i are travelers of time and space lost

THE UNIVERSAL & SUSQUEHANNA MERCY CO. DAYTON, O.

Everybody downtown
Miserable today
Bought the wrong size
Overdrawn at the bank

The spots were there before the leopard
Now explain the panther
Sun reflected in black
Tar pools

"American society"—great dead animal carcase
We try to bury it, forget it
We carve steaks off it and get indigestion
Some of us walk away

Death's ivory
Buck tooth skull
Stone says "I will never live"
Snake: "I'll never die"

All the wrong people rush up to me
Screeching, "You're a poet you're a
Poet you're a Great POET!"
Time to move on. Complete disconnection
Misunderstanding brought on by overpayment

In X-ville California
People swept under the rug
Living sow bug lives
The Dormition of the Virgin
(What a word, also an oil painting or so)
Alice in Wonderland
Bichloride of mercury

Try to reorder your scrambled head & broken eyes
Apply vanilla milkshake anti-paranoia compound
No possibility of escape
Two sets of electrically charged barbwire
The Trojan War continues, the Iliad is unfinished
No sales tax on flame throwers
What's possible? Bandages? Paint?

26:V:72-25:IV:73

George Whitman

THE QUINTESSENCE OF THE EPITOME
for Laura de Los Rios

Among the visions which my memories trace

There is one brightest star, one face

One image from afar, filled with seraphic grace

Each poem is her heart's fantasy

Each flower and tree, is framed within her memory

Each dream, each midnight and each dawn

Are garments thoughts of her put on

Each beam of light from the empyrean blue

Reflects in her the good, the beautiful, the true.

五金杂货

五脏六腑你向我摊出一切 -
锁和各种式样的把手，落满尘土
早已推不开那扇门．这里的陈列
不代表时间的积累，或者
为某种将来的功用，不过支撑
垮下来的自重，干瘪的眼屎，百年
祖屋，虫蛀剩下的感情．
展示一切是为了不给出 -
因为尘土、自重、眼泪和旧爱．
这景象一现，为了必定消失 -
大水将至，蓝色的水位线
画在屋顶：一丝嘲弄，一丝
嬉笑，一对展不开的愁眉．
大水将至．所有的沉积都要
被江水洗净，炸掉，用TNT
然后
再次成为沉积．
为什么不？
八十岁的父亲，六十岁的儿子
肩并肩指给我看孙子建筑的
新城 - 江南春绿，水泥墙，玻璃窗
取代此岸陈旧的木头、虫蛀以及
对往日抽象的温情．
顺流船啊
顺流船
你看我没有退一步的
坚持，眯起眼，用螺丝刀
齿轮，钟表零件的精细
揪心掏肝的冷静．

5/28/01

194

Zhang Er

—Translated from Chinese by the author & *Timothy Liu*

THE HARDWARE STORE

You spread your guts out for me, everything—
knobs and handles covered with dust
unable to open any door for years. Displays
don't present the accumulations of time
or any future function, only sustain
the self-weight crushing down, dried-up sleepy buds, those
hundred-year-old ancestor homes moth-infested,
showing all has been given up
to dust, respect, tears and old love.
Such evanescent displays must vanish
for the flood is coming, blue water marks
painted above the roof: a mockery,
a grin, a pair of eyebrows forever knotted.
The flood is coming. All the accumulated sediment will be
washed clean, dynamited with TNT
then
becoming deposit again.
Why not?
An eighty-year-old grandpa, a sixty-year-old son
standing there shoulder to shoulder, pointing out to me
a new city built by the grandson
high-up on the south shore, spring green, cement walls, glass windows
replacing the wood now rotting on this shore, moth-eaten
and nostalgic
for the downstream boat.
Oh, downstream boat,
you look at me, never stepping back,
insisting, narrowing your eyes like a screwdriver
or a tooth-ripped saw, the delicate interior of a watch
composed as a calmness churns in my guts.

CONTRIBUTORS' NOTES🖋

SAM ABRAMS is the poet at a CIA technical accessory, The Rochester Institute of Technology, where he is tolerated as pirate ship chaplain/clown. He hopes his new book will make him, at last, an intolerable nuisance. He once shared a cell with Benjamin Spock and a joint with Miles. 🖋 **DANNIE ABSE** has written and edited more than 15 books of poetry, as well as novels, plays, and nonfiction on medicine. His *New and Collected Poems* has just been published by Hutchinson. His novel *The Strange Case of Dr. Simmonds and Dr. Glas* (Robson Books, 2002) was published to critical acclaim, as was his autobiography, *Goodbye 20th Century* (Pimlico, 2001). Abse served for many years as a senior specialist at the chest clinic at the Central Medical Establishment in London, where he still resides. 🖋 **GUILLAUME IX d'ACQUITAINE** (1071-1127) is the oldest known troubadour. An infamous libertine in his day, he was excommunicated twice by the Pope for scandalous conduct. As a rich and powerful French warrior, his reach extended far beyond that of the king of France. He assisted Philip I of France against William the Conqueror, erected the Palace of Poictou, and, before his death, conferred large donations on the Church. Of his entire oeuvre, only 11 songs and a musical fragment, all in *langue d'oc*—or old Provençal—remain. 🖋 **LOUIS ARMAND**, awarded the Max Harris Prize for poetry in 1997 (Adelaide, Australia) and the Nassau Review Prize in 2000 (New York state), is editor of the literary broadsheet *Semtext* (Plastic) and poetry editor of *The Prague Revue*. Recent publications include: *Land Partition* (Melbourne: Textbase, 2001), *The Garden* (Cambridge: Salt, 2001), *Inexorable Weather* (Lancashire: Arc, 2001), and *Base Materialism* (New York: x-poezie, 2001). His reviews, critical essays, poetry, fiction, and translations have appeared in numerous journals and anthologies. His work has also been produced on ABC Radio National (Australia), BBC4 (UK), and Radio1 (Prague). 🖋 **JOHN ASHBERY**, born in 1927, is the author of literary and art criticism, a collection of plays, a novel, and more than 20 collections of poetry, the latest one being *Chinese Whispers* (Farrar, Straus, & Giroux, 2002). *A Wave* (1984) won the Lenore Marshall Poetry Prize; *Self-Portrait in a Convex Mirror* (1975), the Pulitzer Prize for Poetry, the National Book Critics Circle Award, and the National Book Award; and *Some Trees* (1956) was selected by W. H. Auden for the Yale Younger Poets Series. The recipient of numerous international awards and fellowships, Ashbery was the first English-language poet to win the Grand Prix de Biennales Internationales de Poésie (Brussels). In 1993 he was made a Chevalier de l'Ordre des Arts et des Lettres by the French Ministry of Culture, and in 2002 he was named Officier de la Légion d'Honneur of the Republic of France by presidential decree. Since 1990 Ashbery has been Professor of Languages and Literature at Bard College. He divides his time between New York City and Hudson, NY. 🖋 **PAUL AUSTER** is the author of a memoir, several collections of essays and volumes of poetry, and 10 novels, including *The Music of Chance* (Viking Penguin), which was nominated for the 1991 PEN/Faulkner Award, and, most recently, *The Book of Illusions*. His *Collected Poems* will be published by Overlook Press in early 2004. He also wrote the screenplays for the critically acclaimed films *Smoke and Blue in the Face* (1995) and *Lulú on the Bridge*

(1998). A former editor of the *Random House Book of Twentieth-Century French Poets*, Auster has translated works by Joan Miró, Jacques Dupin, Jean-Paul Sartre, Stephane Mallarmé, and Jean Chesneux, among others. His honors include the distinction of Chevalier de l'Ordre des Arts et des Lettres, awarded him by the French Ministry of Culture in 1993; the Prix Medicis for foreign literature in the same year; and an American Academy of Arts and Letters Award in 1990. ✍ **IAN AYRES**, founder and editor of *Van Gogh's Ear*, began writing poetry at the age of puberty in houses of ill fame. In 1982, Leona Helmsley fired him from his desk clerk job at Helmsley Palace (New York City) for writing a poem on the back of Elizabeth Taylor's autograph in the hotel's celebrity guestbook. Since then, his poems and short stories have appeared internationally in over 100 publications. In 1999, along with Eric Elléna, he created the movie production company French Connection Films, for which he wrote the screenplay *Killing Your Parents*, currently in pre-production. He resides in Saint-Mandé, France. ✍ **CHARLES BAUDELAIRE** (1821-1867) is widely regarded as the father of modern poetic aesthetics. A French poet, art critic, and translator of Edgar Allan Poe, he is best known for his watershed *Les Fleurs du mal* (1857). This collection of poems broke dramatically from reigning classical conventions and precipitated a legal trial on the grounds of obscenity and immorality. By order of the court, Baudelaire and his publisher were obliged to revise some poems and excise six from future editions. The ban was lifted in May 1949 by the French Court of Appeals. "Le Léthé" is one of the banned poems. ✍ **BILL BERKSON**'s recent books of poetry are *Fugue State* and *Serenade*. A collection of his criticism, *The Sweet Singer of Modernism & Other Art Writings 1985-2002*, is forthcoming from Qua Books in fall 2003. ✍ **ANSELM BERRIGAN** is the author of *Zero Star Hotel*, *Strangers in the Nest*, and *Integrity & Dramatic Life*. He lives in New York City. ✍ **ROBIN BLASER**, born in 1925, is a key figure in the San Francisco Renaissance of the 1950s and early '60s. He moved to Canada in 1966 to join the faculty at Simon Fraser University, where he is now Professor Emeritus. "Recovery of the Public World," an international conference and festival in honor of Blaser's work, was held in Vancouver, Canada, in 1995. The 1993 publication *The Holy Forest* represents his collected poems to that date. Recent work includes the libretto for Sir Harrison Birtwistle's opera *The Last Supper*, which premiered in German at the Berlin Staatsoper in April 2000, then opened in a new English production in Glyndebourne, England, in October 2000 and toured nine cities. Blaser's 75th birthday was celebrated in San Francisco at The Poetry Center in May 2000. ✍ **LEE ANN BROWN**'s new book, *The Sleep That Changed Everything*, was just published by Wesleyan University Press. Her first book, *Polyverse*, won the New American Poetry Award from Sun & Moon Press in Los Angeles. In France, she has been in residence at the Foundation Royaumont and a participant in a conference on American film and poetry at the Centre international de poésie Marseilles. Her most recent work appears in such journals and anthologies as *Java*, *The Baffler*, *The Chicago Review*, and *Best American Poetry 2001*. ✍ **DENNIS COOPER** is the author of *The George Miles Cycle*, a sequence of five interconnected novels: *Closer* (1989), *Frisk* (1991), *Try* (1994), *Guide* (1997), and *Period* (2000). The cycle is published in the U.S. by Grove Press and has been translated into 12 languages. His most recent novel is *My Loose Thread* (2002). *The Dream Police: Selected Poems '69-'93* was published in 1995. He is a contributing editor of *Spin Magazine*, nerve.com, and *Artforum*. He lives in Los Angeles. ✍ **DAVID COPE**'s sixth book, *Turn the Wheel*, will be published by Humana Press in May 2003. Cope was awarded the 1988 award in literature from the American

Academy of Arts and Letters. A veteran of the famed Naropa Institute summer sessions, he was the primary author of their 1990 ecopoetics statement, The Declaration of Interdependence. David lives in western Michigan, where he teaches Shakespeare at Western Michigan University and Grand Rapids Community College. He and his wife of 33 years have three children. ✍ **QUENTIN CRISP** (1908-1999) is the author of the classic and flamboyantly eccentric coming-of-age memoir *The Naked Civil Servant*. The award-winning film version of *Naked Civil Servant* made him an instant international celebrity. Crisp also wrote numerous books and articles about his life and his opinions on style, fashion, and the movies. Often hailed as the 20th-century Oscar Wilde, Crisp was famous for his aphoristic witticisms. He performed his one-man show, *An Evening with Quentin Crisp*, to acclaim in theaters around the world, all the while spreading his unique philosophy: "Never keep up with the Joneses; drag them down to your level. It's cheaper." He was always in the "profession of being." ✍ **GAYLE DANLEY-DOOLEY**, born in 1965, is the 1994-95 National Poetry Slam Champion and the 1996 International Poetry Slam Champion in Heidelberg, Germany. She has written and self-published three books: *Naked*, her first book of poetry; *Soulfull: A Slam Poetry Study Guide for Language Arts Instructors*; and *Passionate: Poems You Can Feel*. Through workshops she calls "SoulSessions," Danley has taught thousands of children and adults to express their innermost emotions through writing and performing their own poems. Gayle lives in Largo, MD, with husband-poet Twain Dooley and their seven-year-old daughter Noni. ✍ **MICHAEL DENNISON**, formerly of New York City, London, Dublin, Omaha, and Baton Rouge, now lives in Pittsburgh, PA, where he teaches creative writing and literature at Carlow College. He regularly performs his poetry with the Ken Foley Trio. His poems have most recently appeared in *Frank* and *King Log*. *Vampirism: Literary Tropes of Decadence and Entropy*, his monograph on vampire literature and disorder, is published by Peter Lang. ✍ **ALBERT FLYNN DeSILVER** has published poems in numerous literary journals, including *New American Writing*, *Zyzzyva*, *Hanging Loose*, *Conduit*, *Volt*, *Slope*, *Fishdrum*, *The Wallace Stevens Journal*, *Web Del Sol*, *Exquisite Corpse*, *LUNGFULL!*, *The Hat*, *Bombay Gin*, *Poetry Kanto* (Japan). He is also editor/publisher of The Owl Press, publishing innovative poetry and poetic collaborations. He is the author of books and chapbooks including *Letters to Early Street*, *Walking Tooth & Cloud*, and *Some Nature*. He lives in Forest Knolls, CA. ✍ **JENNIFER K. DICK**, an American residing in France, has had work or has work forthcoming in such reviews as *Volt*, *Barrow Street*, *The Colorado Review*, *Bombay Gin*, *Stand*, *Frank*, *La Traductière*, and *Tears in the Fence*. Her poems also appear in the anthologies *Short Fuse* (Rattapallax Press, 2002) and *100 Poets Against the War* (Salt, 2003). An art-poetry collaboration, *What Holds the Body*, with Kate Van Houten is forthcoming from Esteppa Editions (France). ✍ **LINH DINH** is a Vietnam-born U.S. citizen who lives in Italy. Writing in English, he is the author of a collection of stories, *Fake House* (Seven Stories Press, 2000), and several collections of poems, including *All Around What Empties Out* (Tinfish, 2003). His work has appeared in several anthologies, including *Best American Poetry 2000* (Scribner, 2001) and *Great American Prose Poems from Poe to the Present* (Scribner, 2003). ✍ **GORDON DOWNIE** is the lead singer and lyricist for The Tragically Hip. *Coke Machine Glow* is his first book and solo recording. Downie lives in Canada and has a dog named Magnet. ✍ **KARI EDWARDS** is a poet, artist, and gender activist. She is winner of New Langton Art's Bay Area Award in Literature (2002) and author of several books and collections of poetry, including *A Day in the Life of P.* (Subpress

Collective, 2002) and *Electric Spandex: Anthology of Writing the Queer Text* (Pyriform Press, 2002). She is the poetry editor for *I.F.G.E's Transgender-Tapestry*. Her work has been exhibited across the U.S. at such venues as the Denver Art Museum, the New Orleans Contemporary Art Museum, and the University of Massachusetts, Amherst. edwards' work can also be found in many journals and anthologies. ✍ **MARK EWERT** is a Capricorn who lives in the turret of a beautiful Victorian mansion in San Francisco. He is currently working on a book (tentatively titled *Beatboy*) about hanging out with Allen Ginsberg, William Burroughs, et. al., when he was but a lad. Ewert wishes to thank poet Tim Dlugos posthumously for the poem "Brian and Tim," from which Ewert cribbed the format for the poem that appears in these pages. ✍ **RUTH FAINLIGHT** has published 12 collections of poems in England and the U.S., as well as short stories, translations, and libretti. Her most recent collection is *Burning Wire* (Bloodaxe Books, 2002). Born in New York City, she lived mostly in England since the age of 15. An Italian *Selected* is due out this summer, and the bilingual English-French collection *Encore la pleine lune* was published by Editions Fédérop in 1997. Her work has also been translated into Spanish and Portuguese. Fainlight is one of the five poets who are the subject of Anne Mounic's critical two-volume work *Poésie et mythe*, published in 2000 and 2001 by L'Harmattan. ✍ **LAWRENCE FERLINGHETTI** was an integral part of the Beat movement, both as a bookseller and publisher of City Lights Press. He is the author of numerous books, including *A Coney Island of the Mind*, which has sold nearly a million copies. A longtime resident of San Francisco, he has served as that city's first poet laureate. ✍ **SUSAN FOX** was born in Akron, OH, and left as soon as she could. She taught at the City University of New York, spent several years in Paris and Rome, and now lives in the French countryside. Her poems have appeared in *Poetry, Boulevard, The Paris Review*, and many other journals. An opera to her original libretto about a hidden child during World War II made its semi-professional debut in New York City in 1995. She has had a screenplay on another Holocaust story optioned and recently completed a novel on that same story. ✍ **ALLEN GINSBERG** (1926-1997) published his first volume of poetry, *Howl and Other Poems*, in 1956. *Howl* overcame censorship trials to become one of the most widely read and translated poems of the century. A member of the American Academy of Arts and Letters, recipient of the medal of Chevalier de l'Ordre des Arts et Lettres by the French Ministry of Culture in 1993, and co-founder of the Jack Kerouac School of Disembodied Poetics at Naropa Institute—the first accredited Buddhist college in the Western world—, Allen Ginsberg authored over 32 books of poetry, prose, and photography in his lifetime. ✍ **SARA GOODMAN** has been writing poetry since the age of 10. Her early exposure to the genre may be traced back to her mother's reading aloud to her all of her own favorites. An undergraduate student in creative writing at SUNY Purchase, Goodman is currently studying abroad at Charles University in Prague, where she is shaping plans to launch a new spoken word series. ✍ **THICH NHAT HANH**, a Vietnamese Buddhist monk, poet, scholar, and peace activist, has written more than 75 books of prose, poetry, and prayers. Driven into exile from Vietnam for his efforts to reconcile North and South Vietnam during the war, Hanh (or "Thây" {"teacher"}, as he is known to followers) came to France, where he founded the Unified Buddhist Church in 1969. Through his work in Vietnam, France, the U.S., and beyond, he has championed a movement known as "engaged Buddhism," which intertwines traditional meditative practices with active nonviolent civil disobedience. His lifelong efforts to generate peace and reconciliation moved Martin Luther King, Jr., to nominate him for the Nobel Peace Prize in 1967. Hanh teaches, writes, and gardens in Plum Village, France, a Buddhist monastery for monks and nuns and a mindfulness practice center for lay people. ✍ **ALAMGIR HASHMI** is the premier Anglophone poet and scholar living and working in Islamabad, Pakistan. Among his many publications are 10 volumes of poetry and several volumes of literary criticism. He has won a number of national and international awards for his work. For three decades he has taught in Europe, Asia, and the U.S., as a professor of English and comparative literature. ✍ **LINDA HEALEY**'s poetry, fiction and reviews have appeared in magazines in France, the U.S., Britain, and Ireland. Her most recent work combines the written word with improvisation. ✍ **LYN HEJINIAN**'s most recently published books of poetry are *Happily* (2000), *The Beginner* (2002), and *Slowly* (2002), which together compose an untitled trilogy. *The Language of Inquiry*, a collection of her essays, was published in 2000. She lives and works in Berkeley, CA. ✍ **AMY HOLLOWELL** is an American poet and journalist who has lived in Paris for 20 years. Her work has appeared in a variety of publications in Europe and the U.S., including *Big Bridge*, *LUNGFULL!*, *Pharos*, *Shambala Sun*, *Tricycle*, and the *International Herald Tribune*. ✍ **AMY HOLMAN** is a poet and prose writer in New York City. She teaches writers how to navigate the literary marketplace and get published, and directs the publishing seminars at Poets & Writers, Inc., a national nonprofit. Holman has twice been nominated for a Pushcart in poetry and is anthologized in *Best American Poetry 1999*. Her poetry also appears in *CrossConnect*, upcoming issues of *American Letters & Commentary* and *Rattapallax*, as well as the animal rights anthology *And We the Creatures*, from Dream Horse Press. ✍ **BOB HOLMAN** is curator of the *People's Poetry Gathering*, *Poetry Guide* at www.about.com, Visiting Professor of Writing at Columbia University, and proprietor of the Bowery Poetry Club in New York City (www.bowerypoetry.com). ✍ **D. J. HUPPATZ,** based in Melbourne, Australia, has published a wide variety of writing, including poetry, literary criticism, and fiction, as well as articles and reviews on contemporary art. His critical and creative writing have appeared in the literary journals *Sulfur*, *Tinfish*, *Aught*, *Heat*, *Meanjin*, *Southerly*, and *Overland*. He is the author of four chapbooks: *The Week Sonnets*, *Sealer's Cove*, *American Songs*, and *City of Swallows* (all by Textbase Publications). In 1998 he co-founded *Textbase*, a literary journal and experimental small press (www.textbase.net). ✍ **MICHAEL HUXLEY**, since his STARbooks' debut in *Fever!* (2000), has contributed significantly to the STARbooks anthologies *Seduced 2*, *Wild & Willing*, *Fantasies Made Flesh*, and *Saints and Sinners*. A published poet and former contributor to Denver, Colorado's groundbreaking *Out Front*, Huxley's work will soon appear in *A View to a Thrill*, edited by Paul Willis. Having accepted the position of Editorial Director at STARbooks Press in April 2002, Huxley now finds himself dying for the sins of writers and guest editors on a full-time basis. He resides in Sarasota, FL, with his long-time spouse Paul Marquis. ✍ **FRED JOHNSTON** was born in Belfast, Northern Ireland, in 1951 and founded Galway's international literature festival in 1986. He is now founder-manager of the Western Writers' Centre in Galway, in western Ireland. He has published two novels, a collection of stories, and eight volumes of poetry, including *Paris Without Maps*, a recent sequence. Among other work, Johnston has translated poems by Michel Martin. ✍ **NIKKI D. KATHERINE**, an educator (PhD) and museum professional, uses history, music, dance, food, and culture to "edutain" and help people/communities to share the stories that help shape our present. She has worked for schools, museums, and cultural institutions and has written a series of African American history articles for two newspapers. She is at work on her first novel. ✍ **ELIOT KATZ** is the author of three books of poetry, including *Unlocking the Exits* (Coffee House Press, 1999). He is co-founder of the literary journal *Long Shot* and co-editor of *Poems for the Nation* (Seven Stories Press, 2000), a collection of contemporary political poems compiled by the late poet Allen Ginsberg. He is also co-editor of the bilingual anthology, *Changer l'Amérique: anthologie de la poésie protestataire des USA* (Le Temps des CeRises and Maison de la Poésie Rhone-Alpes, 1997). Katz worked for many years as a housing advocate for Central New Jersey homeless families. He currently lives in New York City. ✍ **JOHN KINSELLA**'s *Peripheral Light: New and Selected Poems* is forthcoming from W. W. Norton in fall 2003. He is Professor of English at Kenyon College and a Fellow of Churchill College, Cambridge University. ✍ **TIMOTHY LIU**'s first book of poems, *Vox Angelica* (Alice James Books, 1992), received the Norma Farber First Book Award from the Poetry Society of America. His subsequent books of poems are *Burnt Offerings* (Copper Canyon Press, 1995), *Say Goodnight* (Copper Canyon Press, 1998), and *Hard Evidence* (Talisman House, 2001). Tenured at William Paterson University, Liu makes his home in Hoboken, NJ. Liu is the translator of Zhang Er's poem "The Hardware Store." ✍ **LISA LUBASCH** is the author of *To Tell the Lamp* (Avec Books, forthcoming 2004), as well as *Vicinities* (Avec, 2001) and *How Many More of Them Are You?* (Avec, 1999), which received the Norma Farber First Book Award. Her translation of Paul Eluar's *A Moral Lesson* will be published by Green Integer Books. She lives in New York City and is one of several editors of *Double Change*, a web journal dedicated to French-American interaction in poetry. ✍ **GERARD MALANGA** recently co-produced a double CD of selected music by Angus MacLise (Sub Rosa, Brussels, March 2003). He is currently at work on the manuscript for a book of poems tentatively titled *"Who's There?"* ✍ **ROBERT MARX** is an American journalist and poet who has lived most of his adult life in Europe. He tries to maintain a sense of humor to deal with what is coming next in these postmodern times. He recently published a book, or rather a slim volume, *Short Poems* (Publibook, 2002). ✍ **PANSY MAURER-ALVAREZ** was born in Puerto Rico in 1951 and raised and educated in Pennsylvania. She has lived in France and Switzerland since 1973, pursuing post-graduate studies at the University of Zurich and working as a teacher and translator. Her poems have appeared in numerous publications in France, the UK, and the U.S. Her collections are: *Lovers Eternally Nearing* (Editions Thomas Howeg, 1997) and *Dolores: the Alpine Years* (Hanging Loose Press, 1996). A new collection is forthcoming from Hanging Loose. She is a contributing editor for *Tears in the Fence.* ✍ **MICHAEL McCLURE**, a poet, novelist, essayist, and playwright, published his first book, *Passage*, in 1956, a year after reading at Six Gallery. He has produced 16 books of poetry, six collections of essays, two novels, and 10 plays, including the Obie-winning *Josephine the Mouse Singer* and the notorious *The Beard*, shut down by police 14 consecutive nights in Los Angeles. He is also co-writer, with Janis Joplin, of "Mercedes Benz," and professor at the California College of Arts and Crafts. Michael McClure lives in the San Francisco Bay Area hills with his wife, sculptor Amy Evans McClure. ✍ **TRACEY McTAGUE** was born in Brooklyn, NY, where she still lives. Some of her recent work can be read in *Torch, Can We Have Our Ball Back?*, *Brooklyn Stoop*, and *LUNGFULL!* She is currently at work on a project that applies the Cantometric and Choreometric studies of Alan Lomax to her particular folk region of Brooklyn. ✍ **SYLVIA MILES**, the gutsy stage and film actress, started out at the Actors Studio, then moved on to Broadway, where she played fairly conservative roles...until the off-Broadway production of Jean Genet's *The Balcony*, where she allowed a man dressed as a judge to whip her—but only after she forced him to lick her foot! This kind of material packed quite a wallop in 1960, and established Miles as an exciting personality. In 1969, Miles was nominated for an Oscar for her role in *Midnight Cowboy*, in which she outhustles would-be hustler Jon Voight following an athletic and sometimes amusing sex scene. Her second Oscar nomination was for *Farewell My Lovely* (1975), in which she played a boozer with something to hide from detective Phillip Marlowe (Robert Mitchum). She has also appeared in many other films, including *Wall Street*, *She-Devil*, and *Denise Calls Up*. ✍ **DREW MILNE** lectures in English at the University of Sussex. He is currently preparing the book manuscript of his doctoral thesis, *A Critique of the Philosophy of Modern Theatre*, and is editing a reader on Terry Eagleton. He also co-edits the journal *Parataxis: Modernism and Modern Writing* with Simon Jarvis. His collection of poems *Satyrs and Mephitic Angels* was published this year by Equipage. ✍ **MARILYN MONROE** (Norma Jeane Baker), born in 1926, personified Hollywood glamour with an unparalleled glow and energy that enamored the world. But she was more than a '50s sex goddess memorialized in Elton John's famous tribute "Candle in the Wind." Married in succession to childhood neighbor Jimmy Dougherty, baseball superstar Joe DiMaggio, and playwright Arthur Miller, Monroe began as a model and became an actress, completing 30 films in her lifetime and earning a Golden Globe for Best Actress in a Comedy for her role in 1959's *Some Like It Hot*. The 36-year-old Monroe was found dead at her Brentwood, CA, home in the early morning of 5 August 1962. ✍ **EILEEN MYLES** is a poet who lives in NY and a novelist who teaches fiction at UCSD. Author of the novel *Cool for You* (Soft Skull, 2000) and lots of poetry, including *on my way* (faux press, 2001) and *the out-in-a-second Skies* (Black Sparrow, 2001), Myles is now working on a novel called *The Inferno* and is just completing a libretto called *Hell*. ✍ **ALICE NOTLEY**, born in 1945, married the writer Ted Berrigan in 1972, with whom she had two sons. After Berrigan's death in 1983, she married the British poet Douglas Oliver and relocated to Paris, France, where she now lives permanently. Notley has published more than 20 books and has been an important force in the eclectic second generation of the so-called New York School of poetry. Her *Selected Poems* was published in 1993. Her book-length poem *The Descent of Alette* was published by Penguin in 1996, followed by *Mysteries of Small Houses* (1998), which was one of three nominees for the Pulitzer Prize and the winner of the *Los Angeles Times* Book Award for Poetry. In April 2001, Notley received The Shelley Memorial Award from the Poetry Society of America, and in May 2001 she received an award in literature from the American Academy of Arts and Letters. Her most recent book is *Disobedience* (Penguin, 2001). ✍ **JOYCE CAROL OATES** is a recipient of the National Book Award, the PEN/Malamud Award for Excellence in Short Fiction, and the Bram Stoker Award from the Horror Writers of America. She has written some of the most enduring fiction of our time, including *Broke Heart Blues*; *Black Water*; *Because It Is Bitter, Because It Is My Heart*; and the national bestsellers *We Were the Mulvaneys* and *Blonde,* the latter nominated for the National Book Award. Oates is the Roger S. Berlind Distinguished Professor of Humanities at Princeton University and has been a member since 1978 of the American Academy of Arts and Letters. She lives in Princeton, NJ. ✍ **ULICK O'CONNOR** is a biographer, poet, and playwright. He has published three books of poems: *Lifestyles* (1975), *All Things Counter* (1986), and *One Is Animate* (1990). He is well-known for his verse plays in the Noh form, most notably *The Grand Inquisitor*, *Submarine*, and *Deirdre*. His play

Executions broke attendance records when it was produced at the Abbey Theatre in autumn 1985, while two years later, *A Trinity of Two* met similar success. His one-man play *Joyicity*, first presented at the Abbey, was an instant success at the Dublin Theatre and Edinburgh festivals, and enjoyed a packed off-Broadway run in January 1991. O'Connor is a member of Aosdána and is on its Toscaireacht (executive board). *✍* **JOE OKONKWO** is author of the book of poetry *Milk Chocolate/Naked Moon*. He has published in *Priapus Magazine* and *Anthology Magazine*, and online at www.timbooktu.com and www.queerpoets.com. His poem "Ribbons" was poetism.com's Poem of the Day on 1 January 2003. Okonkwo's poem "Speakeasy" appeared in the anthology *Hearts of Glass*. His play *The Adventures of That Brotherman* was workshopped by Edward Albee, and his adaptation of the classic children's book *A Wrinkle in Time* has been produced by Houston's Main Street Theater. As a contributor to *Highnotes*, the e-newsletter of The Metropolitan Opera, his feature articles are read by thousands of Met patrons each month. Okonkwo lives in New York City. *✍* **PETER ORLOVSKY**, born July 8, 1933, in the vanished Women's Infirmary in Lower East Side N.Y., was discharged from Military after telling government psychiatrist, "An army is an army against love." He was portrayed by Jack Kerouac as hospital nurse saint Simon Darlovsky among *Desolation Angels*. He's survived Speed & Junk Hells, sang in jail at anti-war protest & political convention occasions, was published in historic *Beatitude* & Don Allen Anthologies of *New American Poetry*, played Self in early underground Robert Frank Movies, travelled with Dylan's *Rolling Thunder Review*. Orlovsky's books include, *Dear Allen: Ship will land Jan 23, 58* (Intrepid Press, Buffalo, 1971); *Lepers Cry* (Phoenix Book Shop, NY, 1972); *Clean Asshole Poems & Smiling Vegetable Songs* (City Lights Books, SF, 1978). *✍* **JENA OSMAN**'s book *The Character* was published by Beacon Press. She co-edits the literary magazine *Chain* with Juliana Spahr and teaches in the graduate Creative Writing Program at Temple University in Philadelphia. *✍* **BOB PERELMAN** is the author of numerous books, including *Ten to One: Selected Poems* (Wesleyan) and *The Marginalization of Poetry: Language Writing and Literary History* (Princeton). A painting/poem collaboration with Francie Shaw, *Playing Bodies*, is forthcoming from Granary Books in 2003. He teaches at the University of Pennsylvania. *✍* **FELICE PICANO** is the author of 19 books, including the bestselling novels *Like People in History*, and *Looking Glass Lives*. He is also the author with Dr. Charles Silverstein of *The New Joy of Gay Sex* and founder of Sea Horse Press, one of the first gay publishing houses, which has since merged with two other publishing houses to become the Gay Presses of New York. With Andrew Holleran, Robert Ferro, Edmund White, and George Whitmore, he founded the Violet Quill Club to promote and increase the visibility of gay authors and their works. He has won the Ferro-Grumley Award for best gay novel (*Like People in History*), the PEN Syndicated Fiction Award for a short story, and has been nominated for three Lambda Literary Awards. A native of New York City, Felice Picano now lives in Los Angeles. *✍* **PEDRO PIETRI**, born in Puerto Rico and raised in New York City, is a reverend, writer, teacher, poet, and dramatist. He has published 12 books of poetry and plays. *Puerto Rican Obituary* is his most renowned poetry collection, translated into 13 languages by Monthly Review Press and most recently published as an English-Italian bilingual edition in Milan, Italy (Isla Negra Editores, 2000). His most recent publication is *Out of Order/Fuori Servizio* (CUEC {Italy}, 2001). As a playwright, he has staged his work in the U.S. and abroad. He has received grants from Caps and the National Endowment for the Arts; is an alumnus of the New Dramatists; and has served on the governing board of the Poetry Society of America (1985-1989). ✍ **DIANE Di PRIMA** is a poet, teacher, psychic, playwright, healer, magician, anarchist, student of alchemy, and practitioner of Tibetan Buddhism. She is also the mother of five and a grandmother and great-grandmother. Her *Revolutionary Letters* will soon be reprinted by Last Gasp Press with over 30 new poems dealing with our more recent history, and Penguin is publishing *Opening to the Poem* (essays and exercises for beginning poets) next year. Her most recent books are an autobiography, *Recollections of My Life as a Woman: The New York Years*, and her epic poem *Loba: Books I and II.* She lives in San Francisco, where she teaches privately. ✍ **TOM RAWORTH** was born in London in 1938. During the 1970s, he travelled and worked in the U.S. and Mexico, returning to England in 1977 to serve as resident poet at King's College, Cambridge. Since 1966 he has published more than 40 books and pamphlets of poetry, prose, and translations. His graphic work has been shown in France, Italy, and the U.S., and he has collaborated and performed with musicians, painters, and other poets. ✍ **BOB ROSENTHAL** is a poet and a writer. He has co-written and produced five plays. His 1970s *Cleaning Up New York* became a cult classic. His latest collection of poetry is *Viburnum*, published by White Fields Press. Having taught workshops at The Poetry Project, Snug Harbor, and Naropa Institute, he is an adjunct professor of English at New York Technical College. He worked as Allen Ginsberg's secretary for the poet's last 20 years; now serves as a trustee of the Allen Ginsberg Trust; and is currently writing his account on the business of Ginsberg. ✍ **MICHAEL ROTHENBERG** is a poet, songwriter, and publisher of *Big Bridge* online (www.bigbridge.org). He is also author of the novel *Punk Rockwell*. His books of poems include *Nightmare of The Violins*, *Favorite Songs*, and *The Paris Journals*. *Unhurried Vision* will be published by La Alameda Press in 2003. ✍ **SAPPHIRE** is the author of *American Dreams*, a collection of poetry which has been cited by *Publisher's Weekly* as "one of the strongest debut collections of the nineties." Her novel *Push* won the First Novelist Award of the Black Caucus of the American Library Association, the Book-of-the-Month Stephen Crane Award for First Fiction, and the Mind Book of the Year Award (UK). *Push* is published in France by Editions de l'Olivier. Her latest book, *Black Wings & Blind Angels*, is a collection of poetry. On 17 February 2003, Sapphire joined poets from all over the U.S. at the Lincoln Center in New York City to read poems protesting the plans for war in Iraq. ✍ **SOZAN SCHELLIN** taught art education at California State University, Los Angeles, from 1972-1991, when he retired due to the onset of blindness. His poetry has appeared in the *James White Review*. He now lives in San Francisco as a Zen monk ordained by Zenshin Philip Whalen. ✍ **LEONARD SCHWARTZ** is the author of several collections of poetry, including *Words Before the Articulate: New and Selected Poems*, *Gnostic Blessing*, *Objects of Thought*, *Attempts at Speech*, and *The Tower of Diverse Shores* (Talisman House, April 2003). He is also the author of a collection of essays, *A Flicker At The Edge Of Things: Essays on Poetics 1987-1997* (Spuyten Duyvil). He lives in New York City and currently teaches at Brown University. ✍ **SUDEEP SEN** (www.sudeepsen.com) was born in New Delhi in 1964. He studied literature there, as well as in the U.S., and has served as an international poet-in-residence at the Scottish Poetry Library in Edinburgh and a visiting scholar at Harvard University. He has published and edited over 20 books, including *Postmarked India: New & Selected Poems* (HarperCollins), which was awarded a Hawthornden Fellowship (UK) and nominated for a Pushcart Prize (U.S.). Most recently, he's published *Postcards from Bangladesh* and *Monsoon*. His writings have appeared in numerous publications, including the *Times Literary Supplement, Harvard Review*, and *Times of India*. Sen is the Editorial Director of *Aark Arts* and an editor for *The Journal of Commonwealth Literature* and *Six Seasons Review*. ✍ **RON SILLIMAN**, born in 1946, has spent most of his life in the San Francisco Bay Area. He has written and edited 24 books to date, including the anthology *In the American Tree*, which the National Poetry Foundation has just republished with a new afterword. Since 1979, Silliman has been writing a poem entitled *The Alphabet*. Volumes published thus far from that project have included *ABC, Demo to Ink, Jones, Lit, Manifest, N/O, Paradise, (R), Toner, What*, and *Xing*. Silliman is a 2003 Literary Fellow of the National Endowment for the Arts and was a 2002 Fellow of the Pennsylvania Arts Council, as well as a 1998 Pew Fellow in the Arts. He lives in Chester County, PA, with his wife and two sons, and works as a market analyst in the computer industry. ✍ **W. D. SNODGRASS** is the author of several books of criticism, six volumes of translation, and more than 20 books of poetry, from his most recent *Each in His Season* to the classic *Heart's Needle* (1959), which won the Pulitzer Prize for Poetry. Among his many honors are an Ingram Merrill Foundation award and a special citation from the Poetry Society of America. His most recent books are the critical studies: *To Sound Like Yourself: Essays on Poetry* and *De/Compositions: 101 Good Poems Gone Wrong*, in which he re/composes beautiful poems to show readers what makes the original so good. The latter was a finalist in criticism for last year's National Book Critics Circle Award. Snodgrass and his wife Kathy live half the year in Erieville, NY, the other half in San Miguel de Allende, Mexico. ✍ **GARY SNYDER** was born in San Francisco in 1930. He has published more than 16 books of poetry and prose, including *The Gary Snyder Reader* (1952-1998), *Mountains and Rivers Without End* (1997), *No Nature: New and Selected Poems* (1993), which was a finalist for the National Book Award; *Axe Handles* (1983), for which he received an American Book Award; *Turtle Island* (1974), which won the Pulitzer Prize for poetry. He has received an American Academy of Arts and Letters award, the Bollingen Prize, a Guggenheim Foundation fellowship, the Robert Kirsch Lifetime Achievement Award from the *Los Angeles Times*, and the Shelley Memorial Award. He is a professor of English at the University of California, Davis. ✍ **ONNA SOLOMON** moved to France after graduating with a BA from the University of Michigan. She has been in Paris for the past year, living, writing, and working with children with autism. ✍ **SPARROW** (Michael Daniel Gorelick), born in 1953, became a poet in the fifth grade, after reading "The Red Wheelbarrow" by William Carlos Williams. He has published the chapbooks *Test Drive* (Appearances, 1995) and *Wild Wives* (Beet, 1998) and two books: *Republican Like Me: A Diary of My Presidential Campaign* and *Yes, You ARE a Revolutionary! Plus Seven Other Books* (Soft Skull Press, 1996; 2002). His work has appeared in *The New York Times, LUNGFULL!, The New Yorker, Mudfish, The Unbearables Assembling Magazine, The Sun*, and 15 book anthologies. Sparrow's band Foamola has released several tapes, including *May I Take a Bath?* Sparrow himself may be heard on *Family Affairs* (tongue'n'groove), *The United States Of Poetry* (Mouth Almighty Records). He lives in Phoenicia, NY, with wife Violet Snow and 10-year-old daughter Sylvia. ✍ **WILLIAM STRANGMEYER** grew up in Brooklyn, NY, and Old Bridge and New Brunswick, NJ, a product of the post-war nouveau-middle-class and other hyphenations. After unsuccessfully storming academia (as a member of the Royal Del Dracos, D.T.K.L.A.M.F.), he engaged in numerous twilight professions such as barker, cabbie, car-runner, poker-game gofer, grifter, banker, and tile-setter. A 25-year resident of

Paris, he is now an English teacher and translator to pay the rent, and co-editor-in-chief of *Upstairs At Duroc*, a Paris-based literary journal, to soothe his soul and to dance to. ✍ **TODD SWIFT** is a Paris-based poet, (screen)writer, and cultural activist. He is co-editor of several international anthologies of contemporary poetry, including *Short Fuse* and *Poetry Nation*. His own work has been collected in *Budavox: Poems 1990-1999* and *Cafe Alibi* and has also appeared in several journals, including *The Literary Review of Canada*, *Jacket*, *Gargoyle*, and *Poetry Wales*. Swift's spoken word performances have appeared on ABC, BBC, CBC, and RTE, and as part of choreographer Jose Navas' *Sterile Fields* dance piece, from Tokyo to Rio, Montreal to Berlin. In 2002, Swift released the CD *The Envelope Please*, as one half of the duo Swifty Lazarus. He is contributing editor for *Matrix* and poetry editor of the British www.nthposition.com. *Selected Poems* is forthcoming from Salmon, in Ireland. ✍ **EILEEN TABIOS** has written, edited, or co-edited 10 books of poetry, fiction, and essays. Her most recent book is a selected prose poem collection entitled *Reproductions of the Empty Flagpole* (Marsh Hawk Press, 2002). Forthcoming books include *Crucial Bliss* and *I Do: English Poems through Verse, Fiction, Memoir, Correspondence, Performance, Art, and Faith*. Her awards include the Philippines' National Book Award for Poetry, the Potrero Nuevo Fund Prize, the PEN/Oakland Josephine Miles National Literary Award, a Witter Bynner Poetry Grant, and a PEN Open Book Award. She is the founder of Meritage Press (www.MeritagePress.com), a multidisciplinary literary and arts press based in St. Helena, CA. ✍ **JUDITH TAYLOR** is the author of *Curios* (Sarabande Books) and *Selected Dreams from the Animal Kingdom* (Zoo Press). Her poems have been published in the *American Poetry Review*, *Fence*, *Poetry*, *Prairie Schooner*, and the *Boston Review*. The recipient of a Pushcart Prize, she lives and teaches in Los Angeles, and is a founding editor of *POOL: A Journal of Poetry*. ✍ **THOMAS R. THORPE** spent a year in Nepal studying the Tibetan language, simultaneously earning his BA in South Asian Studies from the University of Wisconsin. In New York City he studied graphic design at Parsons; worked as a graphic designer; co-founded the theater company The Dean Street Field of Operation; played drums in Megatherium; wrote articles for and collaborated with CHORUS; and helped produce Tibetan documentaries. Now living in Paris, France, Thorpe continues his forays into film, video, graphic design, music, theater, and poetry. ✍ **NICOLE TOMLINSON** is co-editor of *Textbase* (www.textbase.net), a journal dedicated to experiment/method/process-based writing. Her poems have appeared in *Meanjin*, *Aught*, *Milk*, *Moria*, and *the muse apprentice guild* and are due to appear in *The Prague Revue*. Her chapbook *Familiar City* is currently being scored for performance by composer Tim O'Dwyer. Her new chapbook, *N-Body Simulations*, is forthcoming in 2003. ✍ **EDWIN TORRES** was born in the Bronx in 1958 and currently lives in New York City. He is a lingualisualist, creating text and performance work since 1988. Recipient of The Nuyorican Poets' Cafe Fresh Poetry Award, Torres is series editor of *POeP!*, a bi-annual poetry eJournal, and co-editor of the forthcoming *Cities of Chance: An Anthology of New Poetry from America and Brazil*, both from Rattapallax Press. His most recent work are *The All-Union Day Of The Shock Worker* (Roof Books) and a poetry CD-Rom (Faux Press). ✍ **JOHN UPDIKE** was born in 1932. He graduated from Harvard College in 1954 and spent a year at the Ruskin School of Drawing and Fine Art in Oxford, England. From 1955 to 1957, he was a member of the staff of *The New Yorker*, to which he has contributed poems, short stories, essays, and book reviews. Since 1957, he has lived in Massachusetts as a freelance writer. He is the father of four children and author of over 50 books, of which the most recent are *Gertrude and Claudius*, a novel; *Licks of Love and Other Stories*; and *Americana and Other Poems*. His novels have won the Pulitzer Prize (twice), the National Book Award, the National Book Critics' Circle Award, and the Howells Medal. ✍ **PHILLIP WARD**, writer, poet, artist, and photographer, is the editor of Quentin Crisp's forthcoming book, *Dusty Answers*, curator of the Quentin Crisp Archives (www.crisperanto.org) and executor of his estate. His chapbooks include *Fragmented Images*, *Blue Skies & A Margarita*, and *Winged Flights* (with Jon Howson). His poetry and photographs have been published in various journals and books, including *Priapus*, *Bent Voices*, *Deaf Arts UK Magazine*, *This Way to the Acorns* (edited by Raymond Luczak), *Silence Is a Four-Letter Word* (Luczak), and *GayToday*. One of his Quentin Crisp photographs appears in *The Onion's The Tenacity of the Cockroach* (Three Rivers Press), and another will be the cover photograph of *Quentin Crisp: I'm an Englishman in New York* (June 2003), edited by Richard Connolly. Ward lives in New York City with his partner, Charles Barron. ✍ **PHILIP WHALEN** (1923-2002)—a voice of innovation in American poetry—was born in Portland, OR, on 20 October 1923. Like his college roommate Gary Snyder, Whalen took both poetry and Zen seriously. Celebrated for his wisdom and good humor, Whalen transformed the poem for a generation. His writing, taken as a whole, forms a monumental stream of consciousness (or, as Whalen calls it, "continuous nerve movie") of a wild, deeply read, and fiercely independent American—one who refuses to belong, who celebrates and glorifies the small beauties to be found everywhere he looks. Ordained as an *unsui*, or Buddhist monk, he lived at the San Francisco Zen Center from 1972 until his death. A book of his selected poems, *Overtime*, edited by Michael Rothenberg, was published by Penguin Books in 1999. ✍ **GEORGE WHITMAN** was born in 1913 in Boston. Raised in a family of professors, he chose the life of a hobo. Despite a plan to walk around the world in seven years after graduating from Boston University, he could not carry through, getting stuck in Panama. Whitman was a G.I. in World War II when he ended up in Paris. He fell in love with the city and has never left. He attended the Sorbonne and quickly started collecting books, which he piled high to the ceiling of the hotel room where he lived. People used to visit him in his room to buy books and sit for a chat, much as they do now in Whitman's bookstore. It is at this hotel that he met Lawrence Ferlinghetti. In 1952 he bought the Paris bookstore he runs to this day, christening it Le Mistral. Since renaming it Shakespeare & Co. 10 years later, he has tried to help writers and spread knowledge through the store. ✍ **ZHANG ER** was born in Beijing, China, and moved to the U.S. in 1986. Her writings have appeared in publications in Taiwan, China, and the American émigré community. Her full-length collections are *Seen, Unseen* (QingHai Publishing House of China, 1999) and *Water Words* (New World Poetry Press, 2002). Her poems have also appeared in English in a number of U.S. journals, including *The Five Fingers Review*, *Talisman*, *Tinfish*, and *Poetry New York*. Her chapbooks in translation are *Winter Garden* (Goats and Compasses), *Verses on Bird* (Jensen/Daniels), *The Autumn of Gu Yao* (Spuyten Duyvil), and her most recent: *Cross River . Pick Lotus* (Belladonna Books). She resides in New York City.

ACKNOWLEDGMENTS

Bill Berkson: corrected version of "Signature Song" from *Fugue State* (Zoland Books) by Bill Berkson. Copyright © 2001 by Bill Berkson. Reprinted by permission of the poet.

Anselm Berrigan: "Sabotage" from *Integrity & Dramatic Life* (Edge Books) by Anselm Berrigan. Copyright © 1999 by Anselm Berrigan. Reprinted by permission of the poet.

Quentin Crisp: "Style" from *Dusty Answers* by Quentin Crisp (edited by Phillip Ward). Copyright © 2001 by Quentin Crisp and Phillip Ward. Reprinted by permission of Phillip Ward.

Gordon Downie: "Clouds" and "Lowell, Mass." from *Coke Machine Glow* (Random House Canada/Vintage Canada) by Gordon Downie. Copyright © 2001 by Gordon Downie. Reprinted by permission of the poet.

Ruth Fainlight: "Beetle" and "The Mechanism" from *Burning Wire* (Bloodaxe Books) by Ruth Fainlight. Copyright © 2002 by Ruth Fainlight. Reprinted by permission of Bloodaxe Books and the poet.

Thich Nhat Hanh: "Silence" from *Call Me by My True Names* (Parallax Press) by Thich Nhat Hanh. Copyright © 1999 by Unified Buddhist Church. Reprinted by permission of Parallax Press and Unified Buddhist Church.

Alamgir Hashmi: "*Post Scrotum*" from *Sun and Moon and Other Poems* (Indus) by Alamgir Hashmi. Copyright © 1992 by Alamgir Hashmi. Reprinted by permission of the poet.

Robert Marx: "Poem" from *Short poems* (Publibook, Paris) by Robert Marx. Copyright © 2002 by Robert Marx. Reprinted by permission of the poet.

Sylvia Miles: "Farewell My Dear Friend" from *An Evening For Quentin Crisp* (Westprint, Inc., NYC) by Mary Tahan, Guy Kettelhack, and Phillip Ward. Copyright © 2000 by The Estate of Quentin Crisp. Reprinted by permission of Phillip Ward and the poet.

Marilyn Monroe: "O, Time" and "In the Wind" copyright © Marilyn Monroe, LLC. Reprinted by permission of The Estate of Marilyn Monroe.

Ulick O'Connor: translation of Charles Baudelaire's "Le Léthé" from *Poems of the Damned* (Monarchline/Wolfhound Press) by Ulick O'Connor. Copyright © 1995 by Ulick O'Connor. Reprinted by permission of the poet.

Ulick O'Connor:"Homage to Sean MacBride" from *One is Animate* (Beaver Row Press, Dublin) by Ulick O'Connor. Copyright © 1990 by Ulick O'Connor. Reprinted by permission of the poet.

Joe Okonkwo: "Entitlement" from *Milk Chocolate/Naked Moon* (iUniverse, Inc.) by Joe Okonkwo. Copyright © 2002 by Joe Okonkwo. Reprinted by permission of the poet.

Peter Orlovsky: "America, Give a Shit!" from *Clean Asshole Poems & Smiling Vegetable Songs* (City Lights Books) by Peter Orlovsky. Copyright © 1978 by Peter Orlovsky. Reprinted by permission of the poet.

SUBMISSION GUIDELINES

If you find our journal interesting enough for you to entrust your work to it, we encourage you to subscribe. Our continued existence, and continued ability to read your work, depends mainly on subscriptions. We prefer contemporary, experimental, daring poetry of unusual forms, language genius, and provocation. Submissions should be accompanied by a return address, e-mail address or fax number, and a short biography. Name and address of poet should appear on all pages. Copyright automatically reverts back to the author after publication. Submit up to 5 poems at a time. Previously published poems and simultaneous submissions OK. Cover letter preferred; include SAE with IRCs. Time between acceptance and publication is 6 months. Seldom comments on rejections. Poems are circulated to an editorial board. Published writers receive one free copy of the issue in which their work appears. Spring submission deadline: January 1; Fall deadline is July 1. Submissions should be addressed to: French Connection Press, 12 rue Lamartine, 75009 Paris, France.

PLEASE SUBSCRIBE

You can susbscribe to *Van Gogh's Ear* and become a part of a growing network of poets and readers around the world. Purchase single copies and subscribe online at www.frenchcx.com (secure site; please follow the links). Or, complete this page and send a check in U.S. dollars, payable to "COP-Van Gogh's Ear," to: Committee on Poetry/Van Gogh's Ear, P.O. Box 582, Stuyvesant Station, New York, NY 10009, U.S.A. Checks in euros should be made out to "French Connection Press" and sent to French Connection Press, 12 rue Lamartine, 75009 Paris, France.

The continued existence of *Van Gogh's Ear* is dependent on subscriptions and contributions. Please donate and/or subscribe. Thank you!

I enclose:

_____ $19/19 € (includes postage) for one sample copy, issue no. ____.

_____ $38/38 € for two issues, starting with issue no. ____.

_____ $76/76 € for four issues, starting with issue no.____.

$_____ € donation to keep *Van Gogh's Ear* going.

Name: _____

Address: _____

_____

_____

____

Achevé d'imprimer sur rotative numérique par Book It !
dans les ateliers de l'Imprimerie Nouvelle Firmin Didot
Le Mesnil-sur-l'Estrée

N° d'impression : 1.483.5859